Sex Talks to Girls

LIVING OUT
Gay and Lesbian Autobiographies

Sex Talks to Girls

A Memoir

Maureen Seaton

The University of Wisconsin Press

The University of Wisconsin Press
1930 Monroe Street, 3rd Floor
Madison, Wisconsin 53711-2059

www.wisc.edu/wisconsinpress/

3 Henrietta Street
London WC2E 8LU, England

1   3   5   4   2

Printed in the United States of America

Library of Congress Cataloging-in-Publication Data
Seaton, Maureen, 1947–
Sex talks to girls : a memoir / Maureen Seaton.
p.   cm.—(Living out)
ISBN 978-0-299-22880-4 (cloth : alk. paper)
1. Seaton, Maureen, 1947– .
2. Lesbian authors—Biography.
I. Title.   II. Series.
PS3569.E218S49   2008
813´.54—dc22
2008011971

Some names have been changed to protect the privacy of the individuals described herein.

For my daughters

After going to bed, if you are sleeping alone or with others, just bear in mind that beds are sleeping places. When you go to bed, go to sleep just as quickly as you can.

J. D. Steinhardt, M.D., *Ten Sex Talks to Girls* (1914)

Acknowledgments

I originally intended this memoir as a marker for my thirtieth year of sobriety, a surprise for my daughters on a milestone anniversary. As a practicing poet I actually had little hope of writing past page 3. Therefore, I offer my amazed thanks: to Diane Goodman and A. Manette Ansay, and to Deborah Schneider, all of whom believed in the accomplishment before I did; to Linda Braasch, Connie Hough Cronin, Sarah Gamoke, Pamela Hammons, Gema Perez-Sanchez, Steve Butterman, and Anne Laughlin for their excellent friendship and reads (Annie also recommended it to Joan Larkin, editor of the Living Out series at the University of Wisconsin Press, who, along with Raphael Kadushin at the press, immediately supported it); to Niki Nolin and Cin Salach, my sister artists through much of the writing in Michigan; to Sandra Catlin and Nancy Simmons, proprietors of the Labrys Wilderness Resort at Sleeping Bear Dunes National Seashore; to my family, Jennifer, Emily, and Lori, who continue to adore me no matter which of my secrets I reveal or keep; and, finally, to New Mexicans Beth, Jean, Karen, Prentiss, and especially Marsha, essential goddesses. I love you all.

Sex Talks to Girls

Pre

I'd rather finesse the story of a life, salivate around the edges, not chew on the subject's collarbone, break down her front door and run in and out like a looter. *As a kid I was a cross between a hermit and a bird.* I like metaphor, not the weighty thunk of memory, not—*this is how I lost myself, this is how I got myself back*—an old chest falling down the attic stairs.

There I am on the floor of my boyfriend Danny's apartment circa 1979, Ossining, New York, three years after I quit drinking, a few months after my husband left me for someone more Wall Street, and probably at the spectacular height of a snowstorm. The carpet was scratchy-gray, the stereo a dinosaur overseeing our maneuvers, and my boyfriend's sepulchral roommate who never went out, ever, was oddly missing for the duration of the blizzard. I was thirty-one, miles past the age of sexual initiation, on my back with Daniel above me, and he was doing a fine job of warming me up.

I don't remember how long my hair was (shortish) or how much I weighed (thinnish), but I remember the music we kissed to (The Who) and what Danny said (something about our tongues), and what I did (I did), for it was brand new, although I'd been previously married for ten years to a sexual being (ish).

It was like bleeding from a small cut that suddenly opened and I could see my entire potential, juicy and remarkable, and I just let it pour out. I would soon marry this Hudson Valley boy (my second union, his first)—both of us awkward and introverted—for gratitude and for luck. Even after we divorced, quickly, because of his compulsive gaming (Asteroids), I would remember the gifted geek who tried to save my life by fucking.

One

If this turns into a nun's bar, I'm outta here.

from *Sister Act*

Paradise

At the age of six I sat in my closet in complete darkness, praying for strangers, interceding for ailing animals. Age seven brought me Christ's flesh on a plate, a wafer I carefully swallowed without chewing, and I found myself transported to a lovely place, right off the pew and into something called Paradise. The nuns prodded me back to reality, and I returned, disappointed to be kneeling in the same back-straight position, a chubby little girl with an altruistic bent. I could go from this world to that in less than a second, switch off and swoon out, enter the Passion and hang out there for the entire Lenten season, hunkered down with Mary and the apostles.

At nine I discovered that the dense woods behind our house served a similar purpose. There was an enormous rock about half a mile from our yard. I'd climb to the top and sit there with the oaks. I occasionally packed a small suitcase and took it to the rock with me.

It contained food and a velvet dress I was hoping to grow into. I'd nap there with expectations of deliverance. When I woke up, my heart would find itself still pumping blood, faithful to its private destiny, and I'd feel let down at my continued corporeal existence.

No one seemed to notice I was strange, but for years, until I figured out a way to chemically simulate my own bliss, I was miserable between outings to flying buttresses or soaring trees—I was a girl with a death wish.

The Nun Book

In fifth grade, Mahopac, New York, at a school near the lake where I tried to hold my breath underwater for a full two minutes, my favorite teacher, Sister Alexandrine, told my class about a toddler who was watching her mother peel potatoes one day, laughing and pretending to steal peels off the newspaper. When her mother turned her back for a minute, the child popped a peel in her mouth, choked on it and died right there on the kitchen floor.

The nuns of the Divine Compassion, including Alexandrine the sadist, loved us. They were simply protecting us, nuns' duty—and useful, because my parents were definitely the laissez-faire types, paying little attention when my brother and I ran off for a whole day to sit in an apple tree and eat Macs while we told each other jokes, chewing and laughing our heads off.

Because the Divine Compassions were more preoccupied with death preparedness than the three R's, I was basically self-taught until sixth grade. Then we moved to Long Island and had truly cruel nuns, those dark clichés, who tweaked and pinched, rulered and yanked, using fear to teach us. When I was in eighth grade and my brother in seventh, Sister Robert took him down to the boiler room (a mythical place of fire and justice for all of us children) and spanked his bare bottom with her bare hand.

The atrocities didn't divert me from my persistent daydream, however, my *vocation.* I completely memorized the four-hundred-page epic of convent options I'd cherished since third grade. *Religious Orders of the World.* I'd gone through each entry and systematically eliminated the orders that didn't seem right for me: first, the missionary orders, because I was afraid of earthquakes and tsunamis and believed they only happened in other countries; then the teaching orders—for unconscious, although obvious, personal reasons like Sister Robert.

The nursing orders weren't for me either. I'd happily agreed to visit my friend Maggie's grandfather at a home for the aged, walked confidently in the front door, took stock of the sounds and odors, turned around, and walked right back out. *Stop reading that nun book,* my mother said when I got home and folded into my favorite chair. *Get some fresh air!*

I tearfully crossed out the unattainable entries, from the Sisters of the Sick Poor to the Bon Secours. It was clear to me that the only thing I was any good at was praying.

Elephants in the Basement

My parents' new house in eastern Long Island, right over the Queens border, was fully equipped with its own paradise in the finished basement, ideal inspiration for the start of my life as a saint with a taste for highballs.

My folks were a fun couple when they drank, particularly my father, who partied like a pro most of my life, until he landed head-first on the front lawn, broke his nose, and did a few rather worse things that are more crucial to his story than mine, except to say that he was the first one of the lot of us to stop banging his head against the dam of *Da Nile.* My mother was his sidekick, and I think that was what I, foundling adolescent, mystical fanatic, truly and secretly wanted to be when I grew old enough to pick my own career: somebody fun's sidekick.

Down in our finished basement you could find any liquid you craved to tie one on. I liked that about my parents. We were an authentic drinking family and we attracted serious drinkers. We inherited the outstanding basement from the family who owned the house before us. It was among the main reasons we moved there: the azalea bushes, the speakeasy. My nostalgic parents changed nothing: not the pink elephant wallpaper, garish mirrors, polished wood bar, red stuffed built-in seats—pop decadence preparing us for the apparently whimsical DT's. It was the perfect nursery and I was a genetic landmine. I was a puffy pink sponge. I was cute as a cork.

Body

A couple of years after I'd emptied the local library's shelves of Nancy Drew, Cherry Ames, Trixie Belden, and that red-haired eccentric, Anne of Green Gables—my *kindred spirit*—I looked down at my prepubescent self and realized I still had what a nosy aunt might call my baby fat. The only relative who didn't seem concerned about my bulging tummy and chafed thighs was my father's mother, the solitary source of sweets in my (and my skinny brother's) childhood. She thought I was perfect, pleasingly plump, that an occasional Hershey bar wouldn't hurt me. Her grandmother name was Mom Mom and she obviously trumped my mother, Mom. Although my mother did her best to discredit Mom² and save me from that worst of human fates, a chubby life, she—Mom¹—just came across as kind of mean.

Finally, at age eleven, while I was splitting my spare recreational moments between *Dear and Glorious Physician* (Caldwell) and

Exodus (Uris, not Moses), my mother took me to the family doctor who suggested a diet that shrank me quickly and efficiently and gave me a surprising new habit: not eating.

Mom[1], irrevocably slim herself, was thrilled at my slimmer figure; my father, a young Catholic man of thirty-three, was confused by my developing curves that were finally settling in the right places.

Put on your robe, young lady! (Hysterical Dad.)

I was no longer allowed to appear in front of my one-year-younger brother in my PJs.

The body of a nubile peri-alcoholic is a strange and scary place for its proprietor. Anything I did to it continually, usually with the best, if ignorant, intentions, routinely took on a life of its own, much like repetitive stress syndrome in the musculoskeletal system, only this was in my bloodstream, my nervous system, my cerebral cortex. (*This is your brain. This is your brain without food.*) In short, starving myself altered me enough to feel otherworldly and all-things-possible.

I was a natural at anorexia, which our family doctor called a bad case of "nerves." During my freshman year in high school he prescribed phenobarbital to calm what might have been the last of them. My stomach seemed to start eating itself by most mid-afternoons, and the school nurse would call my mother after someone found me curled in pain on the locker room bench. Mom couldn't come to get me because I had two baby sisters at home, but she'd be waiting by the back door with a spoonful of phenobarb when the bus dropped me off. Those were unusually peaceful times for both of us, she with the spoon of magic green liquid, me opening my mouth like a baby bird, tucking myself into bed then floating about two feet above it.

I only got down to 103 pounds by junior year, although my goal had been to break a hundred. Still, with my twenty-one-inch waist and ribs jutting, I felt almost presentable.

Maggie

I can see now that it was complicated, but at the time, she was simply my best friend who I held hands with and wrote love notes to (and vice versa). For the record: we were no closer to having sex in high school than those two stuffed Piglets over there on my daughter's bookcase. Maggie (Magdalena) put her fingers in her ears and hummed aggressively whenever the word *sex* was mentioned by her mother or any other well-meaner. I knew something about the subject but wasn't extremely impressed. Through most of high school we both wanted to marry Jesus. We planned on entering a cloistered convent together and doing just that. Jesus the bigamist. Ha ha. We didn't care. It made sense to us— the way the Mormon practice of polygamy does to some people and polyamory does to the less patriarchally inclined.

Magdalena's parents were not as fun as mine (they didn't drink), but they were entirely parenty and sane. I stayed over there a lot through high school, as far away from home as legally possible. My mother had kind of flipped out after my two sisters were born, and it seemed like anytime I opened my mouth she'd be chasing me up the stairs with her hairbrush, pushing open my bedroom door, and lowering the boom. She said I had developed a *smart mouth,* and it was definitely her new religion to make me dumb again.

Maggie's bedroom was red and white, a guaranteed slutty color combination according to our art teacher, Sister "Birdie," who told her young charges never to wear red and white together because red reminded boys of passion and white reminded them of bedsheets. Maggie and I thought she was loopy, of course, an alarmist at the least. We'd climb into the double bed at night with our Noxema'd cheeks and our fresh Colgate breath and hold hands innocently until we fell asleep. With our persistent lack of sexual savvy, we were like seven-year-old fourteen-year-olds.

Eventually we were maybe ten-year-old seventeen-year-olds, still nonchalant about bees, birds, and boys, still hell-bent on the God thing. The only possible fervor that rivaled the religious kind for us was music in any form. We were our high school mascot musicians from the time they recognized we could sight-read and, later, that we rocked when we played fourhanded piano. We were excused from classes and study halls to perform together at school events, or to practice for those events, and sometimes we'd just pretend we had to practice and skip class to climb behind the folded up bleachers in the gym to the baby grand and play away. We were like idiot savants who moved through high school on wispy pink clouds, lacing fingers during orchestra practice, bundled in the same white blanket at night.

Cloister

*M*aggie and I spent huge chunks of our junior and senior years on silent retreats in a convent (which no longer exists) on the east side of Manhattan in preparation for the novitiate. The nuns there wore sky-blue habits and looked irresistibly like Mary, our mother-in-law-to-be. They nodded at us as we made pious faces in the hallway, frowned as we cracked up after we passed them. We were notoriously Maria von Trappish. We signed up for hour-long vigils together and tiptoed down to the cavernous church at three a.m. to keep our future husband company. We'd kneel quietly before the monstrance, gently nudging each other awake, earnest fiancées. Then we'd tear back up the five flights to our cells before the ghost hounds in the old church could bite our feet. Mother Jean D'Arc told us we'd have to wait a year or two after high school, gain a little worldly experience in college or the workplace, then the convent would open its arms to us and we would float inside together, never to be seen again.

Campused

Magdalena went off to college in the East Bronx and eloped with a townie in the middle of her first year. They moved to Pennsylvania and had two baby boys in a row. I was the fairy godmother.

I turned eighteen in a Catholic women's college in New Rochelle, New York, where my parents had deposited me on the haunted fourth floor of a gothic dorm so the nuns could restrict my goings-on and goings-out and take away my privileges whenever I screwed up. If I got to the dorm five minutes past 10:15 on a Friday night it meant I couldn't go out past 8:00 the following night. If I was more than an hour late, I was "campused," which meant losing my permissions for a whole month and literally being confined to the college grounds day and night, nose pressed against an invisible electric fence that stretched for miles around the maples, elms, and ancient walls of the college.

Within a few months of being away from parents and parish, my vocation to the convent was flagging so low that I was grief-stricken and went to see the campus priest, Father La Tour. He said kind, wise things to me that resonated throughout my entire adult life but meant zilch to a neurotic teenager. He said that my childhood faith had to be completely destroyed before I could build my own house, brick by brick. When my new faith was finished, he said, it would be strong and truly mine.

I was relieved he hadn't mentioned Hell, but I also didn't believe I wasn't going there now that I'd broken up with Jesus. That was the bitter pill I held in my young hand. I missed my boyfriend Christ. With the toppling of the cloister went the entire sacred scenario, convent wedding to canonization. I still moved through the rituals of Mass, Eucharist, and chastity, but inside I was adrift, I was an apostate, an absconder. I had nothing to protect me from my first and lethal French kiss.

Or reality.

My history professor stood in front of the class and said America didn't belong in Vietnam. Then my religion professor provided us with a litany of theologians that sounded like poetry: Tillich, Kierkegaard, another name I remember only as Diddlybach. I was questioning the nature of God and my country, two simple concepts I'd automatically honored a few months before, and I was terrified that I was headed for destruction like one sow in a herd of sows, a pagan in the Red Sea.

At eighteen I was legal and quickly discovered amphetamines and societally sanctioned alcohol, preferring a wine high to a chemical buzz because it was the closest thing to a God-high I could find. If I wasn't going to marry Him, at least I could simulate His essence. Instead of a nun, I became a full-blown alcoholic.

Weekends

I began to eat again—pretzels, pizza, tuna subs, anything bulky and doughy, with large quantities of milk—to prepare for my nights of drinking. In this way, as with any liability/asset pendulum swinging yin/yang duality, alcohol saved my life.

Ahoy

I discovered my own fun guy at a gin mill a few blocks from campus. The Ship Ahoy was a notorious old man's hangout, but on weekends the college crowd took over—we're talking late 60s—and it shook to Motown, Rolling Stones, Beatles, and Beach Boys. Jimmy Ruffino, a sophomore at our Catholic "brother" school across town, asked me to dance one Sunday night. This was the fun guy who would someday marry my college roommate Ce Ce. Jimmy told me to wait a minute, he was going to go find my future husband (or, as he said, *that asshole*) in the john, and a bunch of us would go to a party together and have more fun. Well, the buddy from the john turned out to be the most fun of the bunch. I'll name him Harper for purposes of disguise and forgiveness (I like the name a lot), and after a whole night of intimate drinking and talking Harper said: *I'll call you.* He was *drunk as a skunk,* as he used to say, and I was in *l-u-v.* I called home and told my parents: *I just met the boy I'm gonna marry.*

Jesus H.

Harper broke up with me after only three months because I was a daily communicant. He would come to pick me up at my college across town from his college, park his mini school bus (his day job) outside the campus chapel, and wait for the 5 p.m. Mass to end. I couldn't seem to stay away from my trip down the rabbit hole, that little white wafer, *Jesus H. Christ,* as Harper called Him. *It's me or Him,* Harper'd say, full of nineteen-year-old bravado, though he must have known that someone whose pronoun begins with a capital letter would have an edge on a mere college boy.

For me it was Mass on weekdays at five and 7&7s (rye and 7 Up) afterward. I was still straddling the faith fence, my soul was in grave danger, and parishioners back home were saying whole rosaries for me—I could feel it.

Harper bartended at the Village Inn on North Avenue as a night job. He could hold his liquor while the others were peeing on their bar stools or puking in the men's room. He'd totter a little, eventually, and grin as if through smog, but I admired his capacity and was grateful for the asthma-earned 4-F status keeping him out of the army, safe and drunk at home. Although I couldn't match him beer for beer, I kept up for a girl, and the seedy old men at the Village Inn called me Mo in admiration.

Then he was gone, at least for the rest of my freshman year. I couldn't have sex with Harper because of Jesus, and Harper got tired of waiting outside the church for a virgin with light pouring out of her orifices and nothing going in.

The Buckboard

I went home the summer between freshman and sophomore
years with two goals: to learn how to smoke so that I'd appear worldly to the rich girls in my school (they never noticed); and to learn how to kiss so I could get Harper back (which I
did). My grandmother took care of the first goal, and a midshipman
named Bruce, who, as it happens, will never appear in this story
again, took care of the second.

Mom Mom, lit Chesterfield in hand: *Hold it like this, Molly, that's
right, now take a little drag, be careful—oh!* (as I predictably coughed
up half a lung) *poor sweetheart.*

I was smoking like her, a veteran, by the end of July, up to a pack
of Marlboros a week by Labor Day.

I have no idea where or how I met Bruce. He might have been an
errant angel, he was so unsubstantial and swathed in light. He had no
last name that I knew of and apparently no parents. He was beautiful

yet asked nothing of me. He picked me up in his Impala and we went to the Buckboard Inn somewhere on Long Island once or twice a week for two months. He ordered pitchers of rye and ginger ale, and he never ever tried to get to whatever base the breasts are. We simply slow-danced and kissed.

And kissed. I told him I didn't know how and he just took me on.

The Buckboard Inn, Johnny Mathis, Bruce: that's it. That's the whole memory, complete as a novena, quiet as smoke coming out of a nose.

Treno Street

*T*n college we differentiated between the potheads and the
alkies, something any young self-respecting addict or alcoholic would laugh at now. We divided ourselves up, this
whole big group of kids Harper and I hung out with from our re-
spective schools, but we were collegial about it most of the time, and
we'd often get together and party across our differences. This was
how I came to dance barefoot in the snow down Treno Street.

It was the heyday of drug busts, cops throwing open apartment
doors, someone yelling *Raid,* kids scattering out windows, toilets
flushing. It felt fresh and terrifying like Bonnie and Clyde or early
Christianity. Harper and I loved our booze too much to regularly
risk arrest for unsettling, mellow marijuana grown on someone's
back porch. Personally, pot took me from zero to a thousand too
fast—wham. At least I could see the wall coming when I drank
wine—or the facsimile of a wall with the illusion of a door. In other

words, I preferred the predictable depression of ethyl alcohol to the paranoid munchies of fragrant hemp, although I sometimes made exceptions to my own rule.

We were Catholic kids away from the altar for the first time—caught in the middle of a war in Asia we were just learning to question. We loved our bohemian lifestyle (moldy stew in the fridge, bleeding gums), our dangerous nights bolting from the College Diner, hanging out of cars on the turnpike, sleeping under the boardwalk at City Island, getting back late to campus and facing the discipline of tired nuns.

One day the whole gang was sitting in the Village Inn, which always felt like a church to me—the shiny wood, the reverence—and a peace march came snaking down North Avenue in the snow in full view through the tinted window. My first antiwar protest and there I was—blobboed.

Harper suggested the group of us go to our friend George's place.

We cut diagonally across the march, yelling and raising our fists in solidarity, to Treno Street, where George had a stash in his attic apartment. We sat around in a loose circle and passed the joint. We were protest dodgers, holed up during a snowstorm with an illegal substance and a gallon or two of burgundy for consolation and Ritz crackers for dessert. Harper and Chiclets had asthma, George was flatfooted, Jimmy was colorblind, and Bob, our unconscientious objector, had convinced the draft board he was a homosexual. All were officially pronounced 4-F.

Some might say we were losers and the girlfriends of losers. We were seventeen, eighteen, nineteen years old.

When I got up to leave no one saw or heard me. Santana was on full blast. Any fear of disturbing the neighbors and risking a raid had vanished, unlike the sagey smoke, which hovered in the shape of a UFO right above our heads. Harper nodded into his wineskin. Ce Ce and Juanita were pretzeled with their guys. I went down the three flights to Treno Street in my stockinged feet and Villager skirt and sweater (both peach) to find the long-over march. I could still hear the chanting in my head. I danced a half mile to the house Harper shared with Chiclets, leaping in the middle of the street, holding my arms up to the snow, blacking out, coming to, loving the snow, loving my body, on fire for peace.

When Harper found me I was asleep on his front porch, approaching hypothermia. My vomit was violent and crimson and lasted for twelve hours. Toward morning, while I momentarily rested my head on Harper's bathroom floor and he gently reprimanded me for smoking pot with my wine (*You* know *you can't handle drugs, Moll.*), the police busted open the door of George's attic apartment, rounded up the sleeping couples, and took the eight anti-warriors to jail. We all celebrated at the bar when they were released on bail the next day. *To freedom!* we said.

The Purple

I completely missed the seventies. I drank daily to make sure
of it. Went right from wedding Harper in 1968 to breaking
up in 1979, bypassing the rock and roll between, Vietnam,
Watergate, Ford's pardon of Tricky Dick. I think I've got my dates
right, but in those somnambulant years, sloshed and anesthetized, I
didn't write anything down. I'm sure I had sex twice (my daughters),
and I'm sure I was an optimistic caring young woman even as I sup-
pressed both my melancholic and my impotent tendencies with gin,
tonic, and lime. Factoids are a blur. Memory yawns when I prod it.

In the middle of all that agnostic smog, when I was twenty-five
(my hair medium short, my body medium thin), Harper (twenty-
six) and I went on a weekend retreat where we hoped to recapture
the harmony of our honeymoon (banana daiquiris?). The marriage
retreats had started in Catholic circles and then spread to Jewish
circles and eventually into Protestant ones as well. Our friends either

went to the Catholic or the Jewish. We signed up for the Catholic, although Harper and I had seriously "fallen away" with the first wave of disillusioned young apostates. He'd plummeted early—around fifteen or maybe nine. After our first French kiss, I fell away too (scotch sours).

On that weekend retreat H. and I had a classic conversion experience. I realized later that few retreatants needed or even wanted a conversion, but I suppose we must have because we got one. A big one.

First we felt profoundly pummeled by some kind of heaven-flung truth, which of course I can't remember. Then we were struck joyful. Ball lightning volleyed off the walls of our little retreat room. We jumped on top of our beds like kids. We cried so much that when the three couples running the weekend came to get us, we collapsed, ecstatic, in their arms and kept crying right through their final presentation. When they asked us privately if we'd like to train to conduct weekends ourselves, we said yes, so they whistled for a priest and suggested we confess the multitude of sins we'd committed since we'd fallen away (sex), and then receive the Eucharist that night. They said that God had magically slipped in through our sacrament. They drew a pink circle and a blue circle on the back of a mass card and where they overlapped, purple, there He was, and there we were: restored Catholics. After our flatlining and gross impenitence, we were on fire.

Harper's flame sputtered over the next couple of years while he tried to keep up in the New-Agey Christianity à la Molly department (both of us still drinking daily, by the way). I cajoled and inspired and guilted him into joining me in all kinds of endeavors—participating in healing circles, singing at guitar masses, sponsoring refugees. Finally, and not exactly surprisingly, out went Harper's little light. I wasn't sure if he had chosen Caesar or if my God stuff had once again gotten under his skin.

My flame blew larger and threatened to blow our holy sacrament to kingdom come.

Glossolalia

The first time I spoke in tongues I was lying in bed next to
Harper thinking he was asleep. Earlier that evening two
members of our prayer group had come over to lay their
hands on us and conduct a prayer request that H. and I be given the
gift of tongues—the first gift, kind of the kindergarten of gifts (see
1 Cor. 14:1–23, if so inclined). I was pretty excited and Harper seemed
to be into it too.

Marilyn and Bob looked at us intently after the prayer. Nothing.
So they went home and Harper and I went to bed, lying next to each
other like two volcanoes. Harper's mouth had opened so many times
in an effort to say something strange and/or inspired that he was
pooped. I'd failed too but couldn't sleep. When Bob left, he told us
to try saying *Alleluia* over and over and maybe it would lead to the
desired nonsense, so that's what I did, under my breath, after H.
started snoring in the double bed beside me. *Alleluia,* I whispered,

embarrassed even in the dark, feeling silly but hopeful, with no idea as to what might happen.

When it started, it was a shock—a geyser that began in my feet and rose in slow deliberate motion up my body, which was still lying next to Harper, who wasn't asleep after all, but frozen there as the sounds gushed out of me—quietly, but unmistakably the ecstatic gibberish of the Upper Room.

Over the next months and years I could stop and start at will. Even without opening my mouth, I could speak tongues in my mind if I wanted to. It sounded a little like the Jewish Sabbath prayer: lovely and liquidy and totally unrecognizable to me. I knew I wasn't making it up, and I knew it was just the beginning of all the "gifts." Still, it felt like a cross between a new bicycle and an imaginary friend, a secret stone in my pocket. It gave me something concrete to do when someone asked me to pray for them or when I'd go to pick H. up at Scarborough station in the evening and he wouldn't get off the train, or he'd get off the train drunk for the umpteenth time in a row. I couldn't translate the words, but I knew from their warp speed that the person I was praying for, as my husband opened the car door, slid in behind the wheel, and slurred *How wash your day, Moll,* was me.

War Story #1

Harper took me to the New Rochelle Hospital ER and waved good-bye at the elevator to the maternity floor. I sat in the wheelchair they'd brought me and clutched my overnight bag that held my size-nine going-home clothes. I'd only gained five pounds during my entire pregnancy because I'd not only dieted through it but had also managed to stop drinking for the nine months. I'd been terrified of gaining weight.

My family lived nine hundred miles away in Illinois—they'd moved there in '69—so Harper was it for me that night. *I'll be waiting at the gin mill, hon,* he said, meaning the Village Inn, waving and grinning. *Have the doctor call me there. I love you!*

It was 1970: Kent State, "Bridge over Troubled Water." It was All Hallows' Eve. Clio was on her way.

They (I can't remember who—how many, what gender) shaved each and every hair from my indecently exposed birthing zone.

33

They gave me an enema and I wobbled, doubled over, to the bathroom on the other side of the room. They gave me a shot of sodium pentothal and laughed, saying I would soon be telling them classified details about myself. *Truth serum,* they said, and left me to wonder what I would reveal if they pumped me for secrets.

Once, I called out for my mother and registered distinct humiliation. Several times I made an effort to climb over the sides of the crib they'd put me in for my labor. I knew I was making a terrible mess of my birthright ritual.

The medicine took my mind but, unfortunately, not the pain. It made my body spin out wildly, divide into hundreds of little bodies, all screaming (there is no other word), and my mind and tongue, in their separate chambers, could not help.

I didn't wake up until Clio was one day old (or so Harper told me). I woke up again when she was two days old. Harper was there and there were flowers on the table beside the bed, I remember them: yellow roses, my favorite. I woke up when Clio was three days old and, that time, I was holding her and Harper was beside me on the bed. I sat on a pillow because I'd had a raft of stitches, inside and out.

My mother said her hair looks like Buddy Hackett's, Harper said.

I didn't remember seeing Harper's mother.

I had just turned twenty-three the week before. My breasts were bound with cloth because Harper and I had chosen formula instead of breast milk. We didn't want the baby to cramp our style, he'd said, logically. They'd handed me a pill to dry up my milk, but it came in anyway, giving me a big stupid lump in my throat.

The nurse arrived to take Clio to the nursery. I watched her wheel my baby out the door and turn right down the hall.

Ha ha, Harper said. *There goes Buddy Hackett.*

Cone

Harper often told jokes about people who were physically or mentally disabled. One of his favorites was the one about "the retarded boy" who was handed an ice cream cone and smashed it gleefully into his forehead instead of putting it up to his mouth.

Whenever we'd see a challenged child in a park or walking along with his parents, or waiting for a hotdog at a hotdog stand, Harper would make a gurgling sound in the back of his throat as if he were having trouble holding something in, and as soon as we were almost but not quite far enough away, he'd literally explode with laughter. Tears would run down his face and he'd look at me, helplessly.

The Plaza

I was a terrible Wall Street wife. A big letdown for Harper, who was a star there from the moment he quit college and purchased a crisp white shirt.

First of all, I didn't get it. My father had sold things like pizza pies, kitchen cabinets, caps and gowns, *War and Peace*—concrete things you could eat or wear or read, things he could talk about over martinis with my mother. Harper sold bonds—traded them, actually—bonds made out of the mysterious air of numbers and hunches and the luck of a network of people finessing deals over the phone. It started below Chambers Street in a virtual community (pre-Internet) with pretend money, huge amounts of it. It was an exclusive game for *qualified* boys, and in those days (as in these days), the boys were rich and getting richer. Harper hopped into the game at twenty-one and told me: *I'll be a millionaire by the time I'm thirty!* More than anything, he wanted to strap me into his fantasy.

I wanted cats and parakeets. A horse. A million dogs and kids. I was a mommy from my first doll onward. I used to save earthworms after it rained when they'd be squirming on the sidewalks of Long Island to get back into the grass before the sun dried them to jerky. I made my own whole-wheat rolls and fresh yogurt and alfalfa sprouts and planned to adopt orphans from war-ravaged places and give Harper's bonuses to charities or to random people, the way John Beresford Tipton did.

I was an activist all through high school. I could pick steel strings like Woody Guthrie. I could do the jerk, the skate, the cha cha, and the shimmy. And there I was married to *The Man*.

As his bonuses grew, Harper wanted a bigger house and a little foreign car he'd been pining over forever. One Christmas week he took me to the Plaza Hotel and we stood at our window high above the city and I heard a voice from my left shoulder: *All of this can be yours.*

I feel bad that I never asked him for a ride in his toy car. Not that bad. It kept breaking down anyway. It was in the shop more than it was on the road. When Harper sat in the driver's seat (I'm getting way ahead of the story now for the sake of this last image) it looked like Mr. Toad's Wild Ride, Harper's head a dot on the map of Westchester.

Bad

I watched a movie where *bad* girls escaped from boarding
school and dove headfirst into an empty in-ground pool.
The fake black ketchup blood was enough to teach me
about consequences. I was nine or ten, not too young to learn a sig-
nificant lesson.

When I found out I was pregnant with our second child I was
twenty-seven. Our old fertility doc, whom I'd gone to see for my
yearly check-up after enduring every test imaginable in those days,
reopened my file, wrote *SUCCESSFUL* across the first page, and
called to tell us the astonishing news. *Due: January.*

Our adoption caseworker (who'd unwittingly approved the ap-
plications of two practicing alcoholics—two nuts who actually
thought they could raise more kids—or one nut who thought she
could and one who found it less of a hassle to acquiesce) was understanding, but told us we would not be able to adopt a child now that

I was pregnant. She was sure, however, that she would be able to find another home for the baby boy who had just been born the day before. Coincidentally, she called us right after the doc did. In one day, I lost a newborn and gained a fetus. I was exhausted.

Harper hadn't come home the night before (off on a toot), and I was very upset when he walked in, disheveled and still high, at 10 a.m. Clio was at nursery school and I could hear myself breaking my own peace and quiet rule. It may be the only time I can remember in our ten-year marriage that we had a shouting match. Then the doctor called with his surprise, and I suddenly and absolutely didn't care if Harper had flown to Vegas in a blackout or taken the train to Quebec to visit the shrine of Our Lady of Hopeless Drunks. The fetus was inside me, not him. I looked at him with his hung-over, hangdog face, and I knew I didn't give a flying fuck what he'd done or would ever do again.

I had nine months to change my life. I didn't think this, but I knew it. Everything that had happened before, except Clio, had been bullshit. I also didn't think that, but my unconscious self was suddenly using profanity and I liked it. I drove to the Hudson at Scarborough station and sat for a long time until I felt my unborn child's enormous soul arrive inside me and my own timid soul leave on the next train out.

War Story #2

Five years after my first war story I'd thoroughly drilled myself in various ancient childbirth practices resurrected by women in the '60s and '70s, and had been triple warned about the still rampant American birthing machine by La Leche League, Monsieur Lamaze, and the Venus of Willendorf. I was armed for anything that might throw me off course, ready to tai chi with Western medicine, and about as in my own shoes as anyone could be, given my bulk and heartburn.

Harper had tied a decent load on that evening and snored loudly upstairs while I sat in the den absently watching late night TV and timing contractions. I half-watched *The Bob Newhart Show* and then I quarter-watched *Easy Rider,* and after all that humor and violence I decided to name the baby Emily if it was a girl (after Suzanne Pleshette's character on *Newhart*), and Dennis if it was a boy (after

Hopper). We'd changed names so often nothing sounded interesting anymore, and these names, I thought, would work just fine.

At five minutes apart I called my neighbor to come over and watch Clio (we'd prearranged), then woke an instantly panicked Harper to take me to the hospital. I'd decided to wait until after midnight to give Harper the opportunity to sleep off his scotch neat and to give myself as little time as possible to labor in fluorescence. I was using my breath techniques and doing well, impressed by the regular contractions that tightened my stomach into a volleyball then eased away like the tail end of a foghorn. I felt energized and I was determined to have my second child without anesthesia.

Harper was slightly slurry and lopsided but in adequate control of the station wagon as we crawled along icy roads to Phelps Memorial in North Tarrytown, which has since been renamed Sleepy Hollow in honor of Ichabod Crane, who lost his head, apparently, between the hospital and the country club. I was busy timing the waves, and the baby, I liked to believe, was gearing up for his/her descent into life as we know it.

Since H. had attended the Lamaze classes too, he was invited into the labor room with me. But since he was still slightly ripped and hadn't gotten into the whole thing enthusiastically to begin with, I like to believe that the Willendorf Venus (although at that moment I'm sure I was thanking the usual male gods) chose to send me Willa, a woman I knew from the neighborhood who happened to be the nurse on duty that night. Willa threw her arms around me, gave H. a nod, and companioned me humorously through the first stage and into transition.

Transition: Who has ever made this trip, raise your hands.

Men: Think Bunker Hill or some such skirmish lasting one to four hours.

Or skip to page _____. I won't be offended.

Transition is when a human being is forced against its will through the neck of its mother's womb, which up until that moment has been holding the whole works inside so s/he wouldn't fall out, and which (this cervix/neck/formerly bolted door of the Alamo) is not known for its elasticity, unlike the vagina, which, everyone knows, is made of spandex.

The poor head, inching its way through the silently howling cervix, needs a dozen or so strong squeezes to complete the journey (I like to think of transition as the Twelve Labors of Hercules), but the new mother will not remember this manageable statistic, as she has entered the Battle of the Amazons in the Forest of Amnesia, and if she dies during this rarefied time, she will mercifully remember nothing.

I could see Willa darkly and I couldn't place Harper (he may have left for the coffee machine, having sobered up sufficiently to recognize amniotic fluid on his slippers), but suddenly I was ten centimeters and someone was throwing me and Suzanne Pleshette onto a gurney and shipping us down the hallway to the delivery room. It was like I lost my paddle over the side of my boat, and I was speeding through some kind of wormhole in the universe with pain controlling me like the giant pain in the ass it was rumored to be. What the fuck, I might have thought if it was a few years in the profane future—still, I was having my first inkling of what it felt like to be furious.

Push, said the doctor, no sooner had I landed in the delivery room. (When had he arrived? What was his name again? Who cared. Redundant prick.) (You may think this was the pain talking, if you wish.)

And, sure enough, my body pushed, not because I wanted it to, but because he'd said the "P" word and I'd salivated in response. Now *there* was a pain I could remember—a ripping apart of any pleasurable sexual experience I'd ever had (in a former life, perhaps), as my vagina filled with Dennis Hopper's head and almost burst.

Stop, I suddenly heard myself demand. I could feel the steam coming out of my Medusa hair and I was vaguely aware that my good girl image was at stake, but I'd been on top of this Herculean business for eight or nine hours now and no one was going to wreck it for me at the finish line.

I got ready quickly, before the next wave set upon me: *Sit up,* I said to myself (*not* Lie down, *Dr. Divot). Okay, wait. Okay, now!*

I thought, I'm totally conscious and this part doesn't even hurt, which is what I'd been told at Lamaze, which is what I never would have believed if I hadn't felt it myself and I never would have experienced if I'd turned my body over to the hired expert, who was waiting eagerly with a scalpel.

My baby crowned and I eased her out without an episiotomy, and, bless him then for this one small important thing, he laid her on my belly, glowing and bloody, tired and tiny.

A new name filled my mouth, nothing I'd previously considered, one she herself had obviously invented on her way to the planet.

Hello, Sophie, I said, to the wise child who, without a word, would inspire me through the first revolution of my life.

Moment

I was hilariously tipsy in the middle of someone's living room, dancing to the Rolling Stones or the Temptations, when I suddenly realized no one was dancing but me.

I looked around at the ten or twelve couples who were sitting there watching me. They seemed mythical and distorted, like John Cheever characters at a carnival, and I knew.

I knew.

Heineken Lite

*I*f I'd kept drinking and lived, I probably would have been drinking daily between 1976 and now with maybe a few weeks off overall for hangovers. At even three drinks a day, a conservative tally, you could estimate I'd have downed 32,850 glasses of alcohol in thirty years. By the end it would have been white wine, and by the postscript it would have been nothing but André champagne. That's if I had continued with the same aesthetic I ended with in 1976. (I was not what some call a heavy hitter, just consistent.)

My mother came to stay with us for a week after Sophie was born. She brought Heineken for me and a child-sized rocking chair for Clio. She concocted tasty lunches and laid them out on a tray—a bowl of homemade soup (pea, bean, mushroom) and half a grilled cheese sandwich—with a bottle of beer to help my milk production. We'd watch soaps together in the den, snug as junkies. Sophie and I slept and shimmered those first few weeks, Harper hit the Oyster Bar more frequently, and Clio raced in the door from kindergarten to rock her baby sister. My mother, for better or worse, was our unwitting last-ditch glue.

"Zoom"

Here's summer solstice.

7 a.m.: Clio, five years old, wakes up on her own, goes quietly down the stairs to the kitchen, pulls over a chair from the dining room, climbs up on the counter and gets the Cheerios box out of one cabinet, a bowl out of another, a spoon, and pours herself some o's, which she prefers without milk. She takes her cereal into the den and turns on channel 13, PBS, to watch her favorite shows in the whole world except for Mister Rogers, which was later Sophie's favorite and always Clio's least, illustrating the interesting differences in their personalities from a young age.

Sophie, five months, and I are upstairs in my bed asleep. She's nursed through the night, so we're both resting soundly with wine in our bloodstreams.

Harper has left for Wall Street after vomiting into the toilet, a morning rite brought about by teeth brushing, and is walking red-eyed and groggy down to the train station on the Hudson, a young bond trader of twenty-eight who has joined the world of short selling and grown-up golf.

Eventually, Clio gets lonely and urges me out of bed.

She does this several times and I finally drag myself awake. If I've stuck to wine the night before I'm not feeling too bad, just wiped out. If I've done the hard stuff, my head will be cracking open.

Sophie stays in bed a while, a peaceful sodden baby surrounded by pillows.

I hate breakfast so I drink a Tab and chain smoke and wait for lunchtime, throwing clothes in the washer and making a grocery list. I nurse Sophie and we watch *Zoom!* Clio imitates Bernadette's unique forearm and elbow trick—which looks like a butterfly—then goes off to play with her seven imaginary friends from the second season: Bernadette, Leon, Luiz, Danny, Edith, Lori, and Neal. Her scenarios with the Zoomers are extraordinarily complex and realistic. Sometimes I myself can see Leon and Edith in their bare feet and striped shirts making jazz hands and zooming with my daughter in the backyard. I worry about both of us as the dryer buzzes.

Playground, supermarket, pet store (fish, snakes, puppies—only looking), gas. We sing along to *Godspell* in the station wagon. We pull up under the white rhododendron (called Mount Everest) in front of the house. Nothing ruffles us. Our day is always the Niagara River heading toward Horseshoe Falls, but we don't remember that.

Cocktail hour begins for me at five or six. Before Harper gets home I pour a glass of wine and place it and my ashtray near the stove, where I prepare dinner. Clio is at the TV again, Sophie in her playpen. We are under water now and moving in separate slow-mo orbits.

If he's home, Harper is home by seven. He takes two glasses from the freezer and makes us gin and tonics to celebrate summer.

We have a small porch by the rhododendron tree where we drink together and with people who sometimes stop by to share our booze—our in-laws, our real estate lady, a few old friends—but usually we drink alone, Pa and Ma, Ward and June, Gomez and Morticia, depending.

9 p.m.: Clio has a perennial fear of ghosts and devils. She is plagued by the Night Mare who gallops out of her closet and through her little room in a halo of light. I see my body sitting on the side of her bed while we hold hands and pray for the breath of God to help her sleep. I want to climb in beside her and hold her, but there is Harper downstairs who says she's too old, and there are two frosted glasses on the table beside him. My heart is trying so hard to make her safe, but the rest of my body is running out of gin.

Buckeye Battle Cry

When my father suddenly stopped drinking on that 5th of July, 1976, I looked at my mother and said: *Are you stopping too, Mom, just in case?* The four of us had been marching around the house to the Ohio State band the night before, plastered. I've got pictures to prove it, Mom in her long white nightgown with baton and 4th of July accessories, the rest of us falling in step behind her.

Harper and I had taken the kids and flown to Illinois to help my father, who'd actually called and asked us to come. We stayed in the house that morning nursing hangovers while two AA guys visited my father for about three hours on the patio, leaving him a Big Book and a meeting list.

Absolutely not, Mom said. *Why should I?*

Uh . . .

Her last twenty years had to be hell, hiding her tumbler behind the toaster, pretending she didn't care about the illicit liqueurs, the tainted wine spritzers, the C. C. Manhattans of yesteryear, her cut-glass crystal rarely lit with gold.

My father would often say, *There's nothing worse than a woman alcoholic.* (Why did he say this?)

As a sidekick, what was she to do?

Meanwhile, I felt an extremely disturbing physical sensation when I tried to stop my daily Heinekens in solidarity with my father—a trembling inside that I didn't recognize. I'd been breast-feeding Sophie for six months and I thought maybe it was a lactating phenomenon. I even called La Leche League to ask if they knew what might cause the shaking apart, but no one did. It took me years to realize I'd been in alcohol withdrawal.

Harper followed my father into AA in the fall. I started going to open AA meetings on Saturdays with Harper, as his support, and one night I was sitting in the front row beside him when a young woman got up at the podium and told her drinking story. It was the same, more or less, as my drinking story to date, which I had assumed was more of a potential story, the story before the story, so to speak. For a brief insane second, I genuinely thought Harper might have put her up to it to trick me. Then I got hot and uncomfortable and realized that if I ever picked up a glass of wine or a bottle of beer again, it would prove one thing: that I most certainly was an alcoholic, and a woman alcoholic at that.

Harper's new friend Chip came up to me after the meeting, smiled, and said, *You can get off the elevator anytime you want, Molly.* I thought he must be high. His eyes looked bright as two bluebirds flying across the sky.

Bea and Brodie

I took myself as quickly as possible to Al-Anon, quintessential lifeboat for family and friends of alcoholics. Anything was better than admitting I was a drunk. I was a *late bloomer,* as they say, operating subliminally and semiconsciously, as powerless over booze as the young boozehound himself (Harper) — or the old boozehounds themselves, if you consider my parents. I think of the two of them as a basset hound and a French poodle, sitting around a card table with fedoras and cigbutts.

Whata ya got, Marice?

Why, a royal flush, François.

Together: *Bottoms up!*

For the spouse of an alcoholic, powerless meant I couldn't get Harper sober if I tried. Who tried? He was my preferred drinking buddy—why would I want to end the ride? Or dry up my source, for that matter? I don't think I ever bought myself a beer in my entire life.

52

Baby Sophie came to my first Al-Anon meeting with me (Maryknoll, Ossining—Hi, Bea, Hi, Brodie!). To me, at twenty-eight, it seemed like a room of godmothers, and I nursed Sophie and cried for the entire hour. Once a week, me crying, both of us sucking in recovery.

I missed a meeting once because the kids were sick with the flu. I was running from bathroom to changing table when the doorbell rang. There were Bea and Brodie, wanting to come in.

The flu! I said.

But they brushed past me, saying something like *Pish-tosh,* set the kettle on, tucked the kids in, touched their fevered foreheads with magic wands, made me tea, and said, *So how are you, dear?*

Their kindness was such a shock, I think I thought: *Holy Mother of God.*

At least I didn't say *Fine.*

That was a start.

Year of the Dragon

To be perfectly honest, I originally stopped drinking because Harper did. I couldn't just go on chilling Chablis while he sweated out hops and ethanol.

He'd been dry for a month or two and I was sitting across the table from him at Dudley's, nursing a goblet of wine, which would affectionately become known as my *last drink*. H. watched me nurse it, and I watched him watch me. I was determined to leave half the wine, something I'd been told no card-carrying alcoholic could possibly do. It was my birthday.

Are you going to finish that, birthday girl? Harper said, dimples mocking.

Naw, I said, flirtatiously. My gears were grinding. I moved the glass aside and dug at my salmon.

He said: *That's what makes me a drunk and you not.* Smugly. (Or so I imagined.)

At home, a young college girl whose name I've forgotten was tucking Clio into bed and listening for the baby asleep in her crib in the master bedroom. The restaurant was a charming purple stucco down the street from Sing Sing prison and around the corner from Revolutionary Road, where we lived in our historic house with our two little girls and Nam, a twenty-three-year-old refugee who'd arrived in Ossining from Vietnam just in time to see his American host family disintegrate.

I accidentally had my last drink of alcohol in 1976. The year of my second child's birth. The Year of the Dragon. The American Bicentennial. A year of cataclysm and grace.

Saved

Soon after Sophie was born, Harper's father, Jack, came down with cancer and started his decline, ascent, or transition, depending on your faith base. I'd been a *live and let live* kind of Catholic on the whole, even while involved in the Charismatic Renewal. Proselytizing never sat well with me, but seeing Jack suffer was absolutely beyond my endurance, and I thought, just maybe, it might help if he got religion.

The day we arrived in Rhinebeck, Jack was sitting in his favorite chair. He was overjoyed that we'd come to visit, and we tried not to notice that the cancer was coming out of his head in egg-shaped lumps. He was buoyant, asking us questions about our trip up, holding his granddaughters, grinning around at us as if he was the luckiest man in the world.

After Clio and Sophie had been put to bed in their daddy's old bedroom and Harper's Mom was tidying the kitchen, I sat down on the floor by Jack's feet.

Hello, dear, he said.

I thought to myself, how am I going to say what I have to say to a man who has so much at stake, who will be dead soon and has yet to accept God? I said: *I'd like to ask you a personal question, Poppy. Would that be okay?*

Ask away.

Jack had never been a churchgoer, but neither had he flaunted his agnosticism. *Too tired on Sunday mornings,* he'd say with that same silly smile of Harper's. He and Eileen had raised four biological, one adopted, and a dozen or more foster kids on a milkman's salary. He loved them fiercely, as he loved his granddaughters and *me,* his middle son's young wife.

Would you like to ask Jesus to come into your heart? I asked.

Sure.

He closed his eyes and waited.

That was the moment I had hoped for. The moment when I would have forged ahead and sincerely said my prayer of intercession for Jack, that his path home be made clear, his pain lessened, that he be transformed and open to being saved. That was the very moment. And it was a thousand years long.

There I was at the feet of a man who had been incredibly ill for two years, who'd lived with such reverence for his own life and ours that he had accomplished that trick of the dying you hear families and friends talk about: unconditional acceptance, something I believed only possible of saints.

I look back now and I know what it means to be changed by a Spirit so holy it has no name. No lineage. No affiliation. No provisos. There I was at the feet of a man who was closer to light than I had ever come in my well-meaning arrogance, my fear-clutched faith; who, right before he stepped off the planet, turned around and showed me God.

Deliverance

I seriously questioned my charismatic practice soon after my prayer team misdiagnosed someone with chronic alcoholism, stating that she needed deliverance from an evil spirit and attempting to drive out the nasty little demon for over an hour. It was exhausting and demoralizing for Millicent, the *afflicted,* and I didn't have enough confidence to assert my own diagnosis, which the AMA corroborated—that as much as alcoholism might resemble demonic possession, it's still a disease, pure and simple. Millicent needed healing, not deliverance.

Prayers for deliverance are considered dangerous for the people doing the praying unless they're totally grounded. Even then, you have to be careful to watch your ego and your id. A crafty little bloke like self-loathing can slip in through a cut on your thumb and you're done for (just kidding) (no I'm not).

We prayed over Millicent while she cried her heart out. I could sense the illness, aggressive and life threatening, that unfortunate twist in her DNA. While my five team-members brought the house down on the demon (rum?), coaxing the bugger out, ordering the imp to be gone and never return, I prayed beside their prayer. Millie left with a sad hope and I left with a breeze of a new self-preservatory idea: defection.

Lobsters

*L*obsters are known to molt one or more times a year and are extremely vulnerable to being eaten at those times, even by other lobsters, especially by the egg-bearing female, who grows quite defensive when she's pregnant.

I never got pregnant after Sophie, and the last time I ate a whole lobster was in Dennis, mid–Cape Cod, on a business trip of Harper's, our first genuine nondrinking excursion. I lowered two beauties into a pot of boiling water, melted butter, and fed my husband tails and claws after the kids had gone to bed. I'd murdered lobsters before. I didn't like doing it, but, hell, while I was drinking I ate snails, for heaven's sake. I had, how do you say, gourmandise.

We'd piled the kids and our rusty beach umbrella into the Ford wagon and headed north and east for the cottage on Cape Cod Bay. Harper met with his associates during the day—I think eighteen holes were involved—and I had the luxury of sunbathing and playing with the kids until dinnertime.

Clio got her hair chewed by llamas at the local petting zoo that trip. Not a pleasant memory, Clio surrounded by a crown of llamas, little face perplexed, pigtails disappearing inside llama lips.

More pleasant: Harper must have taken this picture of the girls and me on the front steps of the cottage. We look incredibly happy. Proof of joy.

I don't think I've mentioned the worst way booze affected Harper. Let's call him an armchair critic (or a sloshed husband), and anyone who is so inclined may overhear his lengthy supercilious audio directed at me (*wimp, loser, blah blah blah*). I'd pretty much been saved from those armchair rants since H. put down the scotch, but for some reason, the urge hit him hard at the Cape and he let loose on his reliable old hassock.

It was interesting, the way I reacted without alcohol in my own bloodstream. I stood for a few minutes, looking at his mouth sucking and wheezing, grinding and gritting; then I turned around and walked up the stairs, checked on Sophie, smoothed Clio's hair, tucked myself in, and turned off the light.

The Wild Mouse

*I*t's important to say the hardest things first, but it's also important to gain trust and then do it. When I chose my first sponsor, Bea, I was still in Al-Anon, which I attended once a week for a year before going to my first official closed AA meeting, and it took a while for me to work my way up to telling her things. This is called a *fifth step* and it isn't as bad as it sounds. It comes after the *fourth,* a thorough housecleaning, an inventory of your former life. It hopefully will keep you from drinking again if you're an alcoholic and from trying to either save or murder an alcoholic if you're married to one. It's like confession, but without the penance, and without the word sin.

You're as sick as your secrets, my sponsor used to say.

My most embarrassing secret at the time was that I'd masturbated—just once—right after Clio was born. Harper caught me and got incredibly jealous and pissed off. He said I'd cheated on him. (I can't believe I bought that one.)

I had another secret about the two of us being drunk after his brother's wedding and I didn't want to have sex but I let him do it anyway after I'd told him *no* emphatically and he was too altered to listen. I hate to say it, but that was it for me in the sex department for a long time. I was twenty-one. We'd been married nine months. I never enjoyed sex with Harper again.

When I was telling Bea these things we were in her kitchen in Croton-on-Hudson, and her husband kept coming in and rooting through the drawers. I think he was fixing something outside, maybe his lawn mower. I thought she would ask him to give us privacy, but she just said: *Oh, don't mind him,* and after a while, I didn't.

I've done much worse things since that first fourth and fifth step, and I've done them dry. The year I was trying desperately not to drink for Harper's sake, going to maybe one open AA meeting a week with him in addition to my own Al-Anon meeting, I scared the hell out of myself and five-year-old Clio on several occasions. I'd replaced my daily bottle(s) of wine with a half-gallon of Breyer's Vanilla Fudge. That's a lot of sugar, if you do the math. But it wasn't enough to keep the crazies I'd experience at cocktail hour at bay. It may have even caused a few crazies, that sugar, since I found out later I had a hefty intolerance for the sweet stuff as well as for the wet stuff.

I'd get this physical sensation like someone had pushed me onto a roller coaster. My brain was suddenly sitting in a car on the Wild Mouse, and it ripped me around and around until the end of the ride, when I'd land at the bottom, regain consciousness, and stand in horror at the damage I'd done or almost done.

One time I told Clio to take Sophie upstairs, and I demolished the little rocking chair my mother had given her, throwing it around the room until it smashed on the floor. Mostly, though, I yelled. My nerves had no coating left. They were shot and I knew it. I was an explosive confection.

I'd sit in our den at night and think about Clio. I could hurt her by accident, I thought, and no one would believe how much I loved her. What was going to stop me from driving us all into the river?

A few years later, after the divorce, my parish priest Father Damien counseled me that I should learn how to swear for therapeutic reasons. (Even after the effects of the Wild Mouse dissipated, I couldn't find within me, much less express, what Damien called appropriate anger.) We practiced saying *hell* and *damn* in his office, firsts for me. When I heard a priest say *fuck* I couldn't believe we weren't struck down on the spot. And when I accomplished it myself with my hands over my head for protection, my dead lace-curtain relatives sat up in their graves *tsk tsk*ing.

Eventually I accepted the value of profanity. I taught my daughters that an aptly expressed four-letter word might save a life. I laughed when people used words like *friggin'* to replace the real thing.

Profanity sounded better and better to me as the years went by. After the divorce Clio and Sophie were the only kids on the block with a single parent, and the only ones who were allowed profanity at home, which was Father Damien's bright idea. I decided when and how it was appropriate, and when it might hurt. We didn't use it lightly. We savored it when we used it, congratulating one another on a metaphor well placed. I wanted my girls to grow up without a mouse in their brains that would uncurl someday and morph into the rodent version of Dr. Hyde.

Clio, Sophie, and I loved the song "Mockingbird" by Carly Simon and James Taylor. We'd dance around the living room, bumping butts and holding fake mics. One day Sophie, who was three then, said, *Play* Fuckingbird, *Mama!*

Clio and I laughed so hard we thought we'd fucking die.

The Problem of Pain

Before C. S. Lewis (anecdotally) became less of a Christian apologist, he wrote a series of books that Clio and I adored: *The Chronicles of Narnia.* They were memorable reads for us, although they seriously encouraged our fantasy lives, which were already over the top.

I decided to try one of his nonfiction works, *The Problem of Pain.* Like Lewis, I wanted to find out why God allowed so much bad stuff in a world He Himself had created (supposedly).

One day I found little whip Clio, who was reading before she went to kindergarten, examining the book and zeroing in on the word *Problem.* She'd already read the others and was sounding this one out.

When she got it, changing the long *o* to short, her head snapped up and she looked at me triumphantly.

I know what the problem of pain is, Mommy.

Tell me! I said.
It hurts!

Bedford

My friend Claudia from Chappaqua took me to my first closed AA meeting in Bedford Hills, where Lois Wilson, founder of Al-Anon and widow of AA's cofounder Bill Wilson, still lived. Ironically, I'd been invited to speak the week before at an Al-Anon meeting where Lois was in attendance, and in the middle of my story as the wife and daughter of alcoholics, I finally realized I was a big fat drunk myself. I was the naked emperor! I saw Lois, who lived through the insanity of her infamous husband—his relapses, infidelity, depression—and the meteor that would break my denial hit me so hard I had to grip the podium. I'd been sitting in Al-Anon meetings for a year, not drinking, telling friends I'd surely become an alcoholic if I ever picked up a shot glass again, and the whole time I'd simply been an untreated drunk. Dry as a neck bone. A whole year of tremors and rage and cravings and coffee up the yang. The phenomenon of *white knuckling*.

When Lois hugged me after the meeting, I almost melted into the floor in humiliation. My Charismatic group would say I'd been convicted by the Holy Spirit. People in recovery would say I'd hit bottom. Unquestionably, it was all coming together for me and it wasn't pretty.

Claudia drove me to Bedford Hills for a trio of Sunday AA meetings. They were back to back, open to anyone who had a desire to stop drinking—or, in my case, a desire to stay stopped. I'd been dreaming that President Ford or sometimes the Pips would force my mouth open and pour gin down my throat. I'd fight them off, but they always won, and I'd get rip-roaring drunk in my dream as a result and was not pleased about it. I'd been profoundly losing my sanity when the clock struck five—that skittering in my veins, teeth clenched. Claudia said, *Come on, Molly,* and I climbed into her Subaru and let Claudia take me to Bedford as a drunk in my own right, one in a long line, one of the lucky.

Honor Wins

*H*arper told me he loved Honor on New Year's Eve day. My friend Claudia and I ate Italian that night, convincing the owner of Vinnie's in Pleasantville to stay open because my husband had just told me he was leaving me for another woman. After Harper dropped the ax I'd felt hovering over us for the months of his undisguised torment, I immediately called Claudia. We met halfway between Tarrytown and Chappaqua and I told her all I wanted was eggplant parmigiana.

Come on, she said, *I know the guy who runs the place on the corner.*

It was my own fault, of course. I'd enrolled in Weekend College at Marymount up the hill from our house and asked Harper to watch our kids on alternate Saturdays and Sundays so I could study psychology. I was out a lot at AA meetings, and when I was home I was happy. Harper didn't recognize his bride.

What an idiot, Claudia said, which I think was something she'd wanted to say about Harper for a long time but wouldn't risk it. I'd told her right along that I thought I was losing him. On Christmas Eve day, the kids and I had gone down to Wall Street to meet Harper for lunch at Delmonico's, an annual outing that started early in our marriage. This was my first sober trip to Manhattan, and it was also the first time I saw Honor, although I didn't know it at the time. She was peeking at the three of us from the other side of an open door in his office. She was foreshadowing herself. She told me later that, at the time, she didn't believe she and Harper would ever be together. I registered her face subconsciously that day, and have often thought since how she must have felt wanting him so much while the three of us were right there in the office, flaunting our long years as a family. We were fabulous. Who would ever leave us?

Wynken, Blynken, and Nod

Sophie and I had been a nursing couple for over two years, through the family move from Ossining to Tarrytown and the staticky beginnings of my sobriety. We'd found no legitimate reason to give up the ritual, even though some raised eyebrows at us or cleared their throats, like we were Amish or nudists. It wasn't something either of us thought about during the day. It was simply there at bedtime for about five minutes as Sophie fell peacefully asleep and I had a built-in quiet time. Then I'd go back downstairs to do the dishes, check Clio's homework, and head out the door for AA.

My pint-sized milk supply dried up after Harper left. One evening there were four of us in the kitchen eating meatloaf, the next, a new woman in the car with Harper's retrieved suits and ties. I was suddenly centrifugally occupied, losing all that had been previously battened—a tough time to keep to comforting routines. At night I lay on my stomach on the family room floor and screamed into the carpet. During the day I roboted around, passing for a mommy.

Clio came home from school that spring with her first sex questions. She was in third grade and had overheard some smirky innuendo. I got a kid's book out of the library and we curled up on her bed one evening with Sophie and Hubert (Clio's stuffed lion) and I gave it a try. My own mother had done this well; in fact, I've never run into anyone whose mother did such a creative job of telling them the right things at just the right time.

Remember, Molly, sex is for love. It's for having babies, of course, but most importantly, it's for love. Not bad for a rabid Catholic.

I wanted to go in the same direction with Clio, and I found myself at the love part, having glossed over the actual penis-in-vagina part, although Clio seemed satisfied—and I got genuinely stuck. Harper's absence at that moment was as large as it would ever be again. I was mute in the middle of it and looked helplessly at Clio. Sophie had fallen asleep between us, and Clio, reading the last page of the children's book of sex over again out loud, the part where the man, woman, and baby smile at the reader from their watercolor wash, said: *It's okay, Mama, I love you.*

At eight she took the helm, and the three of us sailed away.

The Deadlies

Out of maybe twenty priests I had personal dealings with along the way, I'd say eighteen were decent, three or four of those outstanding, with a couple of real clunkers thrown in, of course. One perceptive Franciscan (Harper and I met him on our first retreat) finally told me what was wrong with me. After I went to him for confession he said: *None of those things you just confessed are sins, Molly. Your sin is the sin of scrupulosity.*

When I looked it up, I was mortified because it seemed so close to the granddaddy of sins: pride. It meant I thought I was too perfect to take a chance on committing real sins—the seven deadlies, for instance. Take lust. What the hell was that, I often wondered. I kind of still don't know. Or take sloth: absolutely not. Overachiever. I think I came pretty close with gluttony. I ate a pound of raisins once, right out of the box, to replace the sugar in the wine I was trying not to drink. That was my biggest binge ever, and it was definitely my first and last dried fruit binge.

Then there was envy. That comes around once in a while, but it's always canceled out by genuine happiness for the other person. I can't help it. I'm happy with things like stones and sand dollars. Then I began to think that maybe scrupulosity was a lot of people's problem, not just mine. I noticed that some of the women at my AA meetings were what is known as "good girls." That means they err on the side of never erring, which could be a way to try to feel safe. (Safety, by the way, might be the eighth deadly sin.) Grown-up good girls take care of their families, eat the part of the chicken no one else wants, don't buy a raincoat for themselves when they need one. It's an ad nauseam list. The payoff is three-fold: occasional kudos from the taken care of, that safe low profile, and a resulting self-satisfaction that borders on nutzo. I myself was the model wife—you would never catch me nagging, whining, bitching, shrewing, emoting, farting, belching—as long as I drank enough in the evenings to completely anesthetize myself.

Another priest who was important to me was not a priest yet. He was a Maryknoll seminarian preparing for missionary work in Africa. He looked like Howdy Doody, who had been a childhood favorite of mine. He was the supreme listener. His orange head nodding at me made me feel visible.

Harper was already burning up his sorrowful Johnny Cash albums in our last year together when Bradley became my spiritual advisor and, okay, maybe there was some kind of lust going on, but it felt like love to me, and I was in awe that I could feel that for someone besides Harper. Brad went off to Africa and our little band of Charismatics cried at his going away party. No one more than me, although I kept my secret and went home and detoxed from Brad for about two weeks, praying each day to have my unrequited love removed.

Harper left soon after. I'd guess he was tired of my ongoing God affair and his needing sex. In just a few weeks I'd proved myself unsuccessful at both lust and love, and I looked in the hall mirror one day and realized for the first time in my life that I was beautiful.

Two

Saints should always be judged guilty until they are proven innocent.

George Orwell

Sex 101

I discovered my super powers at thirty-one. Father Damien, a trained, if unconventional, behavioral counselor, wanted me to *Go out and have sex* after Harper left in his tiny sports car, and who was I to question God's earthly counterpart? I practiced a few techniques at home on my own while the kids were at school or napping. That was fun, although initially alarming, since I imagined all of heaven openmouthed at my sudden wantonness. Then I went to one of my AA meetings and looked around. Who would agree to have sex with me and not get involved? (This had been Father Damien's inspired idea, both finding someone at the AA meeting and the not getting involved part.) I settled on Thor. He seemed extremely horny to me most of the time. He was a few years older—maybe thirty-six—and a few years sober—maybe five—so I thought he might take me under his wing and give me some lessons—for free, in a manner of speaking.

I asked him casually out for coffee after the meeting and he said sure, but he already looked to me a little like a caged canary or an unsuspecting duck, and although I wasn't experienced enough to recognize them, tiny red flags were popping up all over my conscience, Father Damien notwithstanding.

So, Thor said, trying not to smile at me from across the table at the Ossining diner.

So, I said, Cheshireishly.

I was wondering—getting control of my face so that I would appear sincere and not like the opportunist I was—*would you be interested in having sex with me, absolutely no strings attached?*

And exactly what Father Damien had said would happen did. Thor said, *Sure.* He was dignified, taking my predicament seriously. I have to admit I was unnerved by how fast he responded, but I knew nothing—nothing! about men, sex, dating. I'd been with one man since I was eighteen, and he was perhaps not the most representative. Before that: Jesus.

Thus we began, Thor and I, hiding my car at a shopping center so no one would see us together (I'd been cautioned by my divorce lawyer to be discreet), splitting my babysitting costs. I approached sex clinically. Sometimes I'd catch myself out-of-body, watching us, taking notes, thinking, hmmm, how do you like that—well, well, well. Breaking Thor's heart was the only harsh lesson. Three months after we'd gotten started, we ended up at an AA dance. Thor said: *Now remember, we're not technically together. Dance with whomever you want and I'll take you home.*

So I danced with Daniel, my second husband-to-be. When I was new in AA, Dan had once walked up to me and handed me a pamphlet, *Where Do I Go from Here?* Then he turned around and walked away in his Daniel way, shy and without expectation. I danced with Dan the entire night. I waved to Thor once in a while. He was shooting the breeze with his friends, watching me, sloe-eyed.

80

I felt like Isolde with her two men in tow, and Dan was definitely Tristan. I told Father Damien the romance scoop at our next session and he beamed at me. His brown Carmelite habit rose and fell with paternal pride. He said, *Next we tackle the orgasm.*

Damien Redux

olly, Damien said when my Isolde problems were bearing down medievally—Thor was crying at meetings and Dan was computering obsessively in his apartment—*have you ever thought about women?*

Since I knew what he meant right away, I must have, but not consciously, and absolutely not happily. I immediately went through a mental list of my friends and thought about each one as an object of my sexual affection. Some qualified, most didn't. I knew I could kiss at least one of them and not throw up, so I looked at Damien and blushed. Then he said: *What about your ex-husband, Harper—if you ask me, he's gay too.*

And that's when I suspected Father Damien was a Carmelite with a fetish. Or a gay guy himself, hiding in the cupboard with the vestments, the unsanctified wine, and the unleavened body of Christ.

Puerperal Fever

*H*aving young children while engaged in a personal revolution was mind-bogglingly challenging for me. How did Mary Wollstonecraft (mother of Mary Shelley) do it? I know she died soon after giving birth to the little mother of Frankenstein, but what would she have done if she'd lived?

There I was vindicating my own right to sex, to sobriety, and eventually to sonnets—not the stuff of herstory, more like mystory— and I had two offspring following me around, understandably expecting to be nurtured at a moment's notice.

When Clio was in Mrs. Dolly Payne's first grade class at Park School, Dolly visited me unannounced one afternoon to ask me how I was managing with my extremely bright child, whom Dolly had recently put in charge of Class Reading Time and was sending home with books from her personal collection. It had never occurred to me that my children might be unusual—or unusually challenging—because of their intelligence. It was kind of like when you're surrounded by alcoholics and you naturally think the entire world drinks like maniacs. If you're surrounded by smart people, the same holds true. You lose perspective. So what if they tested in the two percentile, if Clio was a first grader reading on a junior high level and Sophie wrote me letters when she was three? I was still in charge, the one the little small people were counting on, and I wasn't managing as well as I thought I should be, especially in the financial department. Harper said I was smart enough to work on Wall Street. My father agreed with Harper, at least in principle. They were both pushing me (each afraid he'd have to feed us forever if I didn't shape up) to grab the commuter train to solvency.

I'd go out the door to my AA meeting, and Clio would wave good-bye—did she even know I was gone? But Sophie bore the brunt of the nightly separation. She adored our sitter, Darshna, who lived just two houses away on Pine Avenue, but she never got used to my going. She'd write long letters of missing me and the things she did while I was gone—whole pages misspelled in complete phonic logic—until I added spelling rules to my list of suspect things (Matrimony, Holy Orders, profanity prohibition, etc.).

Sometimes I took Sophie with me to meetings, sat her down with coloring book and crayons, made her weak tea and milk, and showed her off to my loving group. But most of the time I needed the meetings to myself. I was holding on by a few threads, and AA kept me holding. My new sponsor reassured me that the best thing I could do for my daughters was to stay sober. Made sense. I just didn't understand why I felt so undone without meetings. *They're medicine,* she said, with her usual fact-facing sagacity.

There's Sophie's puckered face at the storm door, her shoulders held gently from behind by Darshna. I can't hear the wail, but I know how it sounds and I know how it feels.

I went to seven meetings a week for years before I could consider cutting back. Then I went to six.

Three-Year-Old Sophie's Joke, Benny's Diner

SOPHIE: *Why did the elephant go to meetings?*
MOLLY and CLIO: *Why?*
SOPHIE: *To share.*

Benny's Diner

One of the bitter sweets of my newly divorced, hanging-by-a-single-strand lifestyle was my weekly dinner out with the kids at Benny's Diner in Hastings-on-Hudson. I'd order sole and split it with Sophie, Clio would go for the ravioli, and we'd nurse our Harper-less hearts with the food and the games we made up to pass the time before the meal arrived: versions of "I see a color," "geography," and hot and cold games like "I'm an inch tall and I'm hiding in the _____." Since Sophie had just turned three, Clio (eight) and I suspended all rules for her.

Clio's turn: *Antarctica.*
Molly's turn: *Brooklyn.*
Sophie's turn: *Fish!*
Clio's turn: *Canada.*
Molly's turn: *Denmark.*
Sophie's turn: *Grandma!*
And so on.

When we played "I'm small . . ." Sophie always hid in the sugar bowl.

Clio pretended she didn't see Sophie looking right at the bowl while we were guessing.

Another surprising perk of our Harper-free evenings, particularly one without cooking and dishes, was the empty kitchen table, which became a big desk for me and the girls to use to color or draw or write stories. I thought I would try to support us financially by sending stories and articles to women's magazines. I had the insane hope of the novice writer—why not do what I love (at least I thought I would love it) and make a living at it? (Laugh track.) My teacher at Weekend College had told me my paper on *Song of Solomon* was exceptional. My sponsor even said she enjoyed reading my fourth step. Who needed more encouragement than that?

Clueless, I set out to write things I could sell. Before long, stories about new boyfriends and articles about sprouting beans began to shrink before my eyes. I'd scribble a page of text longhand and whittle it ruthlessly down to one paragraph. It would be like a teeny tiny story—a blip, in fact—and I'd sit looking at it and wonder what the hell it was. Sometimes it wasn't even a story—it was a strange amalgam of me sort of talking the way I talked to my friend Claudie about the UPS guy I had a crush on and a description of the shape of Clio's head bent over her homework, or the light on her head, or the light on the UPS guy's clipboard. I showed a few of these *blips*— it was maybe 1980—to a friend in AA who wrote legitimate short stories. She read them, looked up, and pronounced what seemed to me to be an appallingly harsh sentence:

You're a poet, she said.

God help me! I thought.

I was unable to sustain anything beyond a page. I was excruciatingly perfectionistic—*This morning I took out a comma and this afternoon I put it back in again.* (Oscar Wilde.) I had the familiar sinking feeling that had recently accompanied self-recognition—like when Father Damien asked if I had ever thought of sex with a woman or when I read *Alcoholics Anonymous* and knew, on some dark level, that I qualified as a drunk. Now I was someone who wrote poems. (I couldn't even think the word poet.) Who would feed us?

The bug of iambs and similes bit me bad. It made fast rhythms with its little teeth and cheated at scrabble. It sat next to me in the front seat of the Chevy and offered cheap thrills if I'd take my hand off the wheel and jot the lines that flew around like live wires in my head. It gnawed and wrangled until I sat at the typewriter and pecked out blip after infernal blip.

I couldn't stop.

Then I didn't want to.

Walkman

I was raped in my little house on Pine Avenue. This is not meant to be the center of my story, the fulcrum or vortex, the lens through which each chapter is lit up or sepia'd, the essential mystery in this openness. No.

I have never told my children, asleep down the hall on some night of the week in some month of some year of the time of this story with a full moon like now or perhaps the moon was new, the invisible one, the sign of promise—I have never told them who raped me, and I refuse to expose him now, but not, as some might think, to protect him. In actuality it is only to protect myself. I will call him Trent, because he was an ordinary, if completely disturbed, man with an interesting name, and I let him into the house on Pine Avenue and that was my mistake.

I was young for a divorcée, and I'd lost a great deal of weight in the months before, nursing my little one and cutting too many calories, which meant I'd been a chubby girl for a long time and then I was suddenly a young woman in a turquoise bikini. I wore the bikini to sunbathe in the backyard once in a blue moon, which happens when there are two moons in the same moon cycle—they call the second one blue—and I felt reasonably happy with my life. I had a wild and weedy and beautiful backyard, and in the spring and summer I mowed the grass with my new gas-powered mower, which I filled with gasoline and started up myself. The neighborhood kids often came by to play Fisher-Price with my daughters, and although Clio told me recently that if we'd stayed on Pine Avenue she would have been using hard drugs and possibly pregnant by junior high, I loved it there.

Our cat, Sylvia, brought us rats from the brook across the street. She left them as a gift on the top step of the basement, where there were shelves lining the walls that held kitchen stuff, so I'd open the door to get some oatmeal and there'd be a nice dead rat waiting for me. One time: a mother and two babies. This may seem like a handy allegory, but it's true.

One day a friend from AA came over to show me his Walkman, the first one I'd ever seen. The friend's name was Mike Moran. He always said his whole name at meetings, which was against the tradition of anonymity, but Mike was a tireless nonconformist. He was also the first person to give me the sound advice that depression can't hit a moving target, so he'd jump out of bed in the mornings, he said, before it could get him, and he'd keep moving *all day all day all day*. That was how he talked, and he normally moved around like a pinball, and, on this day, the day of the night of the rape, which neither Mike Moran nor I could have foreseen, he handed me the headphones to his new Walkman and sat down on my sofa to wait for my reaction.

For a woman, and I guess for men too, but in reverse, rape is mythical. Lucrece, Ganymede, the Lock. I'd feared it forever, in other words. I wasn't sure if I'd be the one out of three women in this country who would be sexually assaulted in her lifetime, but when Trent came to my door that night and banged on it loudly and I got up to answer it, lifting my body from the rocking chair where I'd been reading, walking quickly to the door so he wouldn't wake the kids, saying, sure, come on in, whatever I could do to keep peace and quiet, everything seemed like it had happened before and I began to move in slow motion. Or, perhaps I simply remember it in slow motion. I'm not sure.

They say 1,872 rapes are reported in the United States daily. The mythmakers.

I knew Trent. We'd dated and broken up. If there was a blue moon, Trent would have given it to me that night. I could see his eyes were moons themselves, that Trent thought his love for me was fathomless, his desire at such a depth that he lost himself there and it crashed in on him. He couldn't hear me, I realized; or, if he heard me, I was part of his myth.

I knew you would say no, he said in a voice far away yet in my ear. *I dreamed it would be just like this,* chilling me to where my bones waited to be shattered. My kids slept as he carried me up the stairs to my bed.

When I was a musician in high school, I spent hours in the music booth at the local library surrounded by Stravinsky and Ravel. Mike Moran had a tape of Jethro Tull in his Walkman and he'd cued it to *Locomotive Breath,* the song where Ian Anderson breathes so loud through his flute you can hear his ancestors. On that day I almost died of music.

Rape Redux

When I told Father Damien about the rape, he was furious with me for letting Trent in the house. *You had to know he was high on something, didn't you?* I'd never seen Damien angry before. I remembered Birdie, the crazy nun from high school, and the wacko warnings she'd given us about not tempting boys and how to keep ourselves pure. I knew instantly that I was, if not totally to blame for the rape, then, at least equally. *I let him in.* This was my mantra whenever I unfroze long enough to think anything.

I waited to tell my new therapist, Marina, until I'd been seeing her for six months and was pretty sure she wouldn't ream me as well. To my surprise, she said that Trent would have gotten in no matter what. That he would have pushed the door open or smashed a window, that there was no way I could have stopped him.

But I wonder. My friend Roxy took karate and broke two boards and got a green belt and has never been assaulted.

I did not report the rape. There was no actual weapon. I had no visible bruises. He was nuts, of course, and most likely high on something, a big muscled guy. I encased myself emotionally like a mummy, and that was that.

A few months later I went to my first women's-only meeting of Alcoholics Anonymous and sat there. The other women (maybe fifteen of them) were older and of the hard-assed variety of drunks in recovery. It was one of the first women's meetings ever organized in New York state.

I told them.

I've been to a lot of AA meetings in my life. You could say maybe seven thousand plus. I've discovered you can pretty much tell those folks anything. But I didn't know that then. When I opened my mouth and out came the rape account, then the part about Father Damien's betrayal, and then I was sobbing, I was simply done with my secret.

Out of the fifteen women in the room that day, all but three or four had been raped. I couldn't have known this, of course; I wouldn't have predicted such a thing.

The women told me their stories.

My life has been a gathering of elegant information. Everything I know has come to me through what I've done and what has been told to me; or, everything known already exists and I have walked through some of it, guessing at significance. When the women had all spoken, we did not hold hands for the final prayer like they do now. Only Californians held hands in those days. The custom didn't reach New York until '79, and then it would start with the young and work upward.

Boogie

The only one of my friends I ever considered kissing was Claudia. That was it, of course; it never went any further than an imaginary kiss for me, partly because I wasn't sure what you were supposed to do with a woman after you kissed her, and partly because it was Claudie, my best friend, the girl I got sober with, my other half, as our friends called her, and they didn't mean as in lover, nor did I.

In my *Healthy Lesbian Fantasies* (Father Damien's bright idea), Claudie and I would hug happily, jump in my car, and sing along with Van Morrison all the way down to Manhattan.

Occasionally, after a weekend meeting, Claude and I would hook up and take the Saw Mill to the 24 Hour Club on the West Side, where you could hear and feel the music after you got in the freight elevator and started chugging up to the third floor. Usually we'd start out dancing together and get cut in on by guys, but sometimes, when we had our pretend lesbian vibe going on, we'd just dance with each other and shrug the guys off good-naturedly. They didn't seem to mind. The 24 Hour Club was a sober club and, except for the occasional tippling infiltrator, people were relaxed, even generous. They said excuse me when they banged into each other, and hi and how you doin'—friendly nontypical–New York kinds of things. Lots of people danced in groups, especially if there was a newcomer in tow. The actual fact of newcomers on the dance floor was one of the best gifts of the gods I'd seen to date. I loved coaxing them out, watching them take their first steps without booze or drugs—then checking back in with them at the end of the night—and they'd be tearing the place up.

I was pretty new myself, of course, but I loved dancing. Mars, my way-in-the-future future lover, used to say it was the black in me, which she often conjured when she thoroughly appreciated something I could do or something I had (for example, my baked macaroni or my ass). Sober dancing was like flying. When you were in your detoxed body and in sync with your partner, it was like Supermaning over the lights of Manhattan with your Lois, or in my case, vice versa. I loved being conscious.

I once asked Claudia if she'd ever thought about kissing another woman and she made a face and vomiting sounds. When I came out as a lesbian a few years later she had a tough time adjusting at first. *Why would you want to bring more pain into your life, Molly?* And she was right about the pain.

She was also, fortunately, wrong.

Bi Mom

After I married and divorced Dan in '81 I moved myself and the kids to Illinois (for the first time) and stayed there one year before returning to Ossining. My life often volleyed between the Hudson Valley and the Midwest—and when I was home in New York, up and down the Hudson like a tugboat (please see map, if lost). My parents had moved to a small town outside of Chicago as soon as Harper and I married, and I made that trip between New York and Illinois dozens of times by car, plane, bus, and train, kids in tow, for short and long recuperative visits.

That Illinois year I was in love with my new friend Jesse and her cousin Jeff at the exact same time. Jeff and I had a little bit of sex for a few months; Jesse and I never got started. Jesse had a master's degree in philosophy and turned me on to Susanne Langer. Jeff was a musician and songwriter and turned me on to things aural and oral. We all huddled together that Midwest winter in a hot-chocolaty miasma of music and feminist theory. I wrote a song with Jeff. I cooked Greek omelets with Jesse. We survived one winter day together—eighty degrees below zero with the wind chill—when a neighbor froze to death in a snow bank between Crystal Lake and McHenry, his blood stippled with Wild Irish Rose.

Clio was in sixth grade at Cary Middle School and, in her observant way, had caught the vibe between Jesse and me and decided to talk to me about it.

Mom, she said, *are you a lesbian?*

How do you know what a lesbian is?

I heard about it at school. It's a woman who doesn't want to marry men. I think Jesse is in love with you.

Why?

She looks at you kind of like she loves you. Plus, she always repeats everything you say to other people, like she thinks God said it or something. So are you a lesbian?

There's nothing wrong with being a lesbian.

I know, Mom. Mom!

No, I'm not a lesbian. I like Jeff, remember?

Oh, yeah. Well, would you tell me if you were?

Definitely.

Okay. Mom?

Yeah?

I wouldn't mind too much if you were a bisexual. Just don't be a lesbian, okay?

When Clio the Inquisitive was four I'd promised her that she could take her red two-wheeler to heaven if she died. Years later, she made me promise that if I died before her, I would not come back and visit her as a ghost, no matter how much I wanted to.

I told her that her daddy wasn't feeling well when he left us and moved in with Honor. Then I told her that he was better but he wasn't coming back and that he would always love her and Sophie as much as his new blonde children.

Sometimes I lied. Sometimes I didn't know I was lying.

I promise I won't be a lesbian.

The truth is tricky.

At a certain age she threw my motherly wisdom and my collective promises into an enormous pot and boiled it all down. That rich half inch, that essence of (mis)information—she kept.

Some Girls

How can you be sure you're a lesbian if you've never had sex with a woman?

This seemed like a reasonable enough question, and certainly the person who was asking it had behaved reasonably on most occasions. Marina, my therapist who had replaced Father Damien after I found the courage to fire him, was a young mother like me, although still married and therefore several degrees more legitimate. She drove a car that looked like a sugary cereal box and she would stiffen visibly whenever I burst into tears over my sexual orientation. I seemed stuck in some weird and maddening universe throughout my thirties. Maddening to me. Maddening to my therapist. Was I, wasn't I? Was I, wasn't I? Who the hell was I? *Don't you enjoy sex with men?* Marina would say. *I know you do—you told me!*

My disaster with horny Thor from the Ossining group had made me realize I was capable of eviscerating someone if I had sex with him, so the last thing I wanted to do was jump in bed with a woman before I was totally sure who I was: straight, lesbian, or, that perceived cop-out, bisexual. The labels didn't count to me. My potentially dodgy powers did.

While I was living outside of Chicago in '81 I went to see the Judy Chicago exhibit of vulvas on plates around a long table—*The Dinner Party*—and was feeling pink and giddy when I walked out onto Printer's Row and noticed the *Some Girls* exhibit across the street. I went in. About half way around the room, I realized I'd walked into a den of lesbian art and I immediately adopted the body language of a sophisticate from New York with a liberal unruffled mind. I strolled as I would have at MOMA. I lingered over certain pieces, bending in, examining, stepping back. I looked around at other women looking at the art, and I pretended I was truly looking at the art. I had never in my life been so close to actual lesbians. I could feel them breathing on me, dousing me with their lesbian breath.

But the acting effort must have freed my psyche, or perhaps the art did, because when I walked out onto the sidewalk it hit me like the punch line of that old alternative-to-tomato-juice commercial, and I practically slapped my own head when I realized: *I should have had a V-8!*

That was how Father Damien would become a prophet. And how his replacement, Marina, came to repeat her reasonable, if rhetorical, question throughout the 1980s, when all I wanted was a woman and all I ever seemed to end up with was a man.

Jamie

One of the first things I told Jamie when we came together in the early '80s (back in New York) was that there was a teensy chance I might be a lesbian. I was hoping I wasn't, I told him sincerely, that I'd never even come close to kissing another woman, but I just wasn't sure so I thought he should know. Basically, I was still worried about my sexual powers and their mysterious ability to level even the most levelheaded of men. I liked Jamie. He seemed incredibly vulnerable to me, like a baby bobcat. I opted for total honesty as the only safeguard. I told him I was thirty-four after he told me he was twenty-nine, that I had two daughters, and that I had a high IQ. Oh, and that I'd decided not to shave my legs for the winter as an experiment against self-objectification.

He had a high IQ himself, he said. He liked older women with kids (my kids liked him best of any of my boyfriends), and he found hair sensuous (notice his own shoulder-length do). He was so completely nonjudgmental and non-nonplussed that I toppled into his budding sex addiction without blinking. My naïve streak was wide and bountiful, a ribbon of misconceptions and blind spots that stretched down 5th Avenue like the rainbow flag on pride day. I didn't know, for instance, that straight men who aren't religious fanatics admire lesbians, at least in bed. I'd never seen a moment of porn in my life, two women sparring with their tongues before a man enters the ring and takes them both down. Nor had anyone ever informed me about the fantasy lives of human males, not to mention their dormant addictions.

And never in a million did I guess that while a woman is struggling with her sexual identity there's a mighty chance the guys she chooses to sleep with will be struggling with theirs as well. In other words, I had no way of knowing that sweet baby Jamie was a freak.

Voodoo

I'd be exaggerating if I said that while Jamie and I were together I thought of our life as Hollywood, but whenever I tried to leave him he would somehow curse me with his solipsistic magic, and I'd abandon my resolve and search for the camera to document the proceedings. I sometimes had the creepy unsettling feeling that if he were a woman he'd have squeezed his menstrual blood into my tomato juice to keep me knotted to the bed sheets.

We were not your typical boy-girl flick stars. I cringed at big screen sitcoms that made my life look like a typo. *Reality is somewhere between them and us,* Jamie used to say when we'd made love and were waiting for the kids to come back from their father's. Who was "them"? I wondered. Jamie lived in the subtleties, a teaspoon of zest, a sprig of rosemary. Reality was a hand-tied fly on a quarter-inch hook, the flick of a wrist over a trout stream. Sometimes he'd say things like: *This is real.* And he'd point to the blue veins of my temples, which fascinated him, or a small spot he'd found at the base of my spine that held a teaspoon of Pepsi when I lay still.

There were plenty of loose theatrical threads around Jamie and me. There were my children, for one thing, shining in and out like suburban lightning bugs. I'd refused to take them to see *Cinderella* or *Grease* because I didn't want them waiting for a prince, yet there I was, hoping my frog would turn into one. *You can't protect your kids from Hollywood forever,* Jamie would say flatly—no panache, no regret.

I used to say that Jamie reminded me of Charles Bronson, but I might have meant Manson. There was a scary pathos about him, although not treacherous, I thought, because no one with Newman-blue eyes could be treacherous. He resembled prey himself, eyes like the martyrs in my old *Lives of the Saints*—Saint Polycarp, chum for the lions; Saint Blaise, who cured a boy found choking on a fish bone, then "lost his head after terrible torments."

Jamie was leaning against a wall at an AA dance when I first felt myself lassoed by his infamous attitude of doom. I was still green as a postulant, trained in courtship by a priest. I said: *Do you dance fast?*

I'd polled my male friends in AA on how to find out quickly, and therefore with a minimum of pain, if someone is interested in you. Tommy C. said: *You can't take it personally if the guy doesn't know you from Adam's house cat.*

My *dance fast* line jetéd above Jamie's head. He did not bite. He stood there looking like the Hudson had dried up and schools of fish were flopping in the air. *Well,* I said, pushing my hand through fog, *do you dance slow?* This one seemed to stop him. A slight tempo-change to the eyes. I wasn't certain of my strategy, but even then I could feel his anchor swaying in the river of my sheltered *slash* brazen life. It groaned prophetically and slipped snugly into place, there in the Hudson Valley, January 1984, the year, according to Orwell, we would all go under.

Sonnet

Those first days, Jamie would drive his Z up to Ossining, park the car facing downhill toward the river, then park himself on my floor and request to hear one of my poems. I obliged and then he'd read to me: Eliot, Miller, Kerouac. *The Boys,* I called them, good-natured disdain apparent, the way the Sisters of the Sacred Heart had taught us girls to indicate superiority. I stretched out on my futon and waited for Jamie to haul his butt across the floor.

It took two weeks, fourteen literati-packed days: Hemingway, Ginsberg, Melville. My kids found Jamie easy, basically unoffendable. Sitting on the floor made him a patient toy or warm-blooded playground equipment for Sophie, who liked to tie and untie his high tops and braid his hippie hair while he read *Moby-Dick.* Alternate weekends the kids were off to Harper and Honor's house, living their Rockwell life, and I had Jamie to myself.

I loved that sex didn't happen right away. I loved listening to his accent, sweet Bronx, his tenor inflection, the way he acted as if sex were epilogue. How blasé can blasé look, I thought, as he sat against the World War II hydrangead walls. Jamie was the Chef of Blasé, an Eagle Scout on my braided rug with lust so far away it seemed buried in the desert, rumbling way out there in White Sands, the beginnings of a nuclear detonation whose idea hadn't yet reached the East Coast. I thought at first he might be waiting for me to make a move. After all, I'd symbolically clubbed him twice at the dance not that long before. Our courtship felt so deliberate, fragile.

On the fourteenth night he finished reading Melville and looked at me propped up on an elbow, floor of peeling turquoise linoleum between us. Then he bit his lower lip in an astounding flash of insecurity and carried that tentative mouth across the ocean to kiss me.

Sleight of Hand

Harper got the kids away from me in '84.

Clio, Sophie, and I were living with Jamie on Eastern Avenue in downtown Ossining. We were crowded but happy. Harper and Honor had just bought a house in Pocantico Hills and fixed up a bedroom for each of the girls. The place was charming, cows down the street in one direction, a chapel with Chagall windows in the other direction. A gingerbread house on Rockefeller's old estate land.

Jamie and I rented an attic apartment where the bedrooms were so small I fixed up Clio's closet for Sophie like a little secret nook, and that was her room. She was seven. Clio, thirteen, was Harper's logical target, susceptible to consumerism and peer pressure. She'd had enough *adventures* with me (as I called them) for a lifetime: attic living, Christmas in the woods, secondhand clothes shopping. She was naturally the one Harper would try to woo away.

The truth was that if Clio left, Sophie would have to leave too—with the child support cut in half, I wouldn't be able to support us anymore. I was working as a teaching assistant in the Walkabout Program (a wilderness training alternative for high school seniors in Westchester County) and bringing home peanuts. Somehow I had to convince Sophie, who wanted to stay with me, to go with Clio. I did it over a period of weeks, persuading her with an invented enthusiasm that made me insane with grief.

Harper couldn't tolerate giving me child support. I knew this. I knew that it made no sense to him to send me money to raise our children when he had a large house and a pregnant wife willing to do it for free. So he pushed for custody from the beginning.

The way he pushed was horrific to me, accusatory and unreasonable, nickling and diming, using the kids as leverage, so out of the blue I often reeled with confusion. At one point he told me he'd go for my jugular if I tried to fight him. He would say things like that—*I'll go for your jugular*—and I couldn't imagine that he hadn't started drinking again, he sounded so much like his old self. I was never sure what he meant, what he had against me, but I couldn't take the chance that he would find out I was having shameless sex with Jamie—or, worse, that I might be a lesbian—and take the kids away forever. He and Honor were a formidable Wall Street couple—they had the money and, obviously, the self-confidence to wear me down. One time Harper told me that it should be obvious to me by now that God loved him and did not love me because he had money and I was poor. (He said this.)

By the time I actually questioned my right to my own children, Harper had won.

After years of fighting, I opened my hands and they slipped away.

Sleight of Hand Redux

I found a shrink in Manhattan who kept me out of the hospital where my anguish had been steadily pushing me. He said: *Make two AA meetings a day, Molly, see me on Wednesdays, and you'll get through this.*

I met Harper at his attorney's office in Tarrytown (I had no legal help myself) and signed the papers they pushed at me from across the polished table, giving Harper custody of Clio and Sophie.

Visitation rights were reversed. Boxes stuffed with toys and clothes were lined up at my apartment door, the kids ready to move into the gingerbread house.

When I walked out of the office that day I could see the Hudson down the hill between the shops and banks of the village. Jamie and I would have more time to ride our bicycles, I thought. I thought: I'll have more time to write.

I didn't know that Clio would be back in a couple of years, crazy for help. Or that Sophie would eventually follow.

I vomited in the parking lot. I sat for over an hour in my car, waiting for God to show up and do something.

Double Scorpio

*J*amie had been married to a woman who left him in their third year and threw their furniture into the street while he was out getting drunk with grief. He had two pedigreed Weimaraner puppies who adored him, and the three of them sat in the window of the Yonkers apartment during the tail end of a hurricane that had caused a flood (the same year Kill Brook overflowed in Ossining) and watched a Sealy Posturepedic mattress Jamie recognized as his and his suddenly-gone wife's rafting down the hill toward the Hudson.

After that he did the series-of-women thing, flailing and falling into the inevitable disillusionment. Some of his dates had kids; one lived across the river, one in the city, one even worked on Wall Street a few buildings away from H. and H.'s office—she was the one he was breaking up with when I asked him if he danced fast and then slow.

Before me, before any of these women, before the wife and the flood and the runaway mattress, he'd been a prostitute.

People keep all kinds of things hidden. And for good reason. Jamie kept things hidden, but not the things one would expect and only those things he himself was not aware of. I asked him what he meant by prostitute—that men gave him money and he did things to them? He said yes but wouldn't say more. It was before he was clean, he said, an old life, one he'd shed more than two years before, a crispy snakeskin. He was a new man now, he said, with healthy new skin, and his eyes rose toward heaven like Saint Sebastian's. He smelled of lime and cilantro.

After our first sex in the hydrangea blossoms under the eaves of the old house, where the landlord lived beneath us and around us like windows everywhere, up the hill from the prison, down the hill from Clio's middle school and Sophie's elementary school, a quick drive to my ex-husband's new home, and for several years mid-decade, Jamie and I evolved into an unsettled, scorpionic, vaguely dramatic couple.

This was how we looked to the world:

Jamie, not tall, not short; rugged (notice hiking boots in summer); hair to shoulders with an inherited gray streak on the right side (like the Bride of Frankenstein); Paul Newman eyes that appeared elusive. He was intimidating, physically strong, quietly charismatic. The only ones brave enough to mess with Jamie were the state troopers.

I, on the other hand, appeared benign to the world at large. State troopers loved me, neglected to stop me no matter how much I violated their limits. Pink freckly female with long dark hair and hazel eyes you had to get close to in order to discern their forecasts. I was round and distinctly non-*Cosmopolitan.* I had been winged painfully in two divorces but was discovering intriguing pastimes while I recouped.

112

Pictures prove we looked appealing together, Jamie's dark halo, my light. I knew from the way we badgered each other, contrasting sides of a clown suit, that we were fatally polarized. In photos I'm smiling and he's not. I have no idea what he looked like grinning; I can't remember his teeth or how he sounded when he laughed. Or if he did.

He must have.

Jamie Dark

One June night Jamie and I set out walking toward each other from opposite ends of the Croton campground driveway, a distance of about a quarter of a mile. The dark was opaque with a stupendous clamor of tree frogs and crickets. We'd both agreed we could not see our hands in front of our faces or each other more than a few inches away. That was the whole point, the darkness a way to access the erotic in our relationship—proof that yin energy could win over fear.

Jamie drove me to the beginning of the driveway, dropped me off, then headed back to its end at the campground. When I heard him kill the engine, I knew he was walking toward me and I started walking toward him. I could see absolutely nothing. The tangled canopy overhead blocked out moon and starlight and I couldn't even see the trees. I had one thing to go by: my footsteps on the blacktop. To either side was the dirt floor of the forest. The road stretched before me in a fairly straight line. I believed that. I believed that Jamie would not double around and scare me from behind. I believed that the nocturnal animals of the forest would not careen into me, deliberately or accidentally. I believed that I could concentrate on my feet and the hard road and that when Jamie and I got close enough, we would feel each other there breathing and that our reunion would be gentle, almost an anticlimax, that the trip through the dark would stay with me for the rest of my life.

And there he was.

Plato's Retreat

*J*amie took me to my first gay pride parade in Manhattan. We arrived late and only made it to the after-parade festivities on Christopher Street. The gay guys were checking Jamie out, and I thought that was fair since I was pretty sure by now that I was going to be a lesbian someday. Lesbians weren't checking me out and I didn't care for the imbalance of attention, but I was philosophical about it. My rising sign tends to make me invisible in a crowd or from a distance. You have to get up close—like in bed or across the table—to realize how cute I am. This is what I've been told.

Jamie was one of those guys, like Thor, who believed he wasn't the possessive type. When I'd told him after a year or so that I was still thinking about the whole sexual identity thing he suggested we bring in a female friend as a companion to our lovemaking and I, totally unashamed of my possessive nature, said no way. Then he suggested Plato's Retreat.

I'd heard about Plato's Retreat, which was somewhere in Manhattan, because a few of the students in my Psychology of Sexuality class had gone there on a field trip at the professor's urging. I chose to do my paper on female sexual dysfunction instead, my old forte, but was fascinated with their reports of couplings and surprised when they said there was no alcohol on the premises. They'd opted to leave their clothes on and just scope the place out. It wasn't necessary to engage in sex, they insisted, but it was fun to watch other people engaging.

I told Jamie I'd give it some thought. He said he was in no rush.

He introduced me to porn as a way of preparing me for Plato's Retreat, although he reminded me that the bodies I would see in real life were much more varied and interesting than the ones in the videos. I liked Jamie's democratic outlook. His aesthetic was completely his own.

I was caught up in Jamie's Plato Retreat plan partly because I was caught up in his sex addiction and partly because I was afraid he'd go by himself if I didn't go with him. Or that he'd cheat on me with a girl we knew in AA who I thought had a crush on me, but come to find out, she had a crush on him. This gay guy from the city also had a crush on Jamie. They were the same height, which has always appealed to me in a couple, and one had brown hair and one had blond, and they were both geniuses. One time I was so jealous of this guy, who told me outright that he planned to take Jamie away from me, that I suddenly wanted to run him over in the parking lot of the Elmsford diner.

Okay, I told Jamie, *I'll go. But just this once—with my clothes on.*

Jamie turned from the porn flick we were watching and made love to me right there on the couch. We never even looked up at the part we both liked—where one woman says to the other: *You look hot, Hilda, are those your new reading glasses?*

Billie Jean

Jamie and I went to Plato's Retreat twice. Once I kept my clothes on and just watched stuff, and the next time I used the tiny towel they provided for cover, like the rest of the clientele, and did some of my own stuff with Jamie. Jamie at Plato's Retreat was like me at a wine tasting. Or like Jamie at a wine tasting, for that matter. After the second time we went I decided I would have to break up with him soon. There was simply nowhere else to go but back for more, and I'd come to the end of my private experiment after I'd accidentally brought a woman with really soft skin to orgasm, thought yup, I'm a lesbian, and then realized I had just heard Jamie ask me to marry him.

I liked the part where a woman stripped on the dance floor to "Billie Jean." I liked that I could walk around half-naked the second time there and not care I was bulging out of my towel.

I hated the paper umbrellas in the cranberry juice they served at the bar. I hated the way we voyeurs looked sideways at one another, pretending to be uninterested. I hated that everyone seemed to be from Jersey. I hated the husband of the woman with the soft skin because he almost fucked me, and I hated Jamie because he was going to let the guy do it and then he was going to do the wife himself. Swinging, they called it. First I'd failed at fly-fishing, and now this.

Jamie was so in love with me that second night. Even though I started crying before the main fucking could take place, he said he saw our potential and it was breathtaking.

Eventually, I would leave Jamie and he would threaten suicide in a small apartment on Highland Avenue where you could hear the TV of the people downstairs so clearly you'd swear they were right there in the room with you, and for that, for the utter powerlessness of the seemingly small situation, you would truly want to hurt somebody.

Z

A shrink I saw a number of years ago suggested that I might have been addicted to the way Jamie smelled. *Like food?* I said, intrigued. The shrink shrugged.

Jamie was a creative designer of culinary treats and the head chef at the prep school where he got me a job as the food service secretary. When we broke up, he made me a no-sugar-added apple pie with my favorite apples, McIntosh, topped it with cheddar, and left it, warm, at my apartment door. Our relationship was punctuated liberally with fresh herbs and lots of garlic. When he wanted to make up for something, he'd prepare dinner for me and sit back and watch me eat it, which always made me nervous, but he insisted he couldn't eat after he cooked, and I knew this was true.

I once wrote the exact same lines as the ones above in a diary entry about Jamie. *A shrink I saw,* etc.—the whole thing about being addicted to Jamie's food odors. I get a strange kick out of that possibility.

I seemed to be addicted to everything else pleasurable, why not that? Jamie smelled like food, what can I say, some days vanilla, others a whole kitchen's worth of spices. I've been trying to figure things about Jamie out for a long time. My AA sponsor used to say, out of kindness, *You can't choose who you love, Molly.* I wonder if this is true.

Jamie had just blown his savings on a vintage Datsun Z when I met him. He was not a materialistic person in the least. What he owned he could pretty much fit in the Z, but he loved his car. We drove to Mystic, Connecticut, that winter. Jamie packed a picnic for us: crunchy bread, olives, brie, melon. He was a faultless lover, a skillful chef, he was sober, and he adored me.

What's not to love, I told my sponsor.

Something was wrong, but she and I couldn't say what. We worked the steps together, trying for the solution.

That spring, some asshole broke into the Z and ripped the whole dashboard apart to get at the radio. Jamie didn't have the right kind of insurance to get it fixed, or else he just lost heart.

One day he hugged me so hard that he injured my back, left side, right beneath my shoulder blade. He took me to the emergency room and they put me on codeine, a drug I'd never had. I was so nuts on it that Jamie suggested we have a ménage à trois with his friend Stan. I finally said yes, but I couldn't go through with it. I went off the codeine right away and endured some kind of record pain for the next six months, during which time I thought for sure I would drink—or at least jump out a window. Claudia told me not to jump out a window because it would be my luck to end up paralyzed from the neck down for the rest of my life instead of dead.

The aforementioned shrink thought that Jamie felt so guilty about this incident (although the hug had seemed innocent) that he could no longer look at me without feeling responsible. I wonder if *this* is true.

What is true is that Jamie is no longer here to defend himself.

Bear

After Jamie came home from his first hospitalization for depression, we set out for the mountains. I have a few blurry instamatic pics of him from this trip. He'd gained much of the weight back and looks at ease. I love these pictures, although in some ways it's like looking at family photos of a benign cousin I've never met. I knew him so long with the angles and the fear—who is this soft-edged man with the blue eyes smiling in the middle of a trout stream in the Adirondacks?

Jamie eventually ended up in a locked long-term facility. He'd performed a couple of Houdinis from earlier hospitalizations and the authorities didn't want to take any more chances. I guess they thought that if they locked him up for a year they could fix him. The first time, he had simply walked away from the local mental ward, and they rounded him up and put him in Stony Lodge. Then he escaped from Stony Lodge. He was so crafty. Lying there in isolation, he realized that the putty around the window next to his bed was fairly new and still a little soft. Over the course of several days he used his plastic fork to scrape away enough of the putty to remove the window, and he simply climbed out and dropped to the ground. Then he went to the first phone he could find, which happened to be at a local bar less than a mile away, and called me.

I'm out, he said, and I could tell he thought I would be glad.

Then he told me to hold on and I heard this on the other end of the line:

Excuse me, sir?

Yes, officer?

Have you seen this man?

A pause, while Jamie looked at a picture of himself distributed to local police by Stony Lodge.

No, officer, I'm afraid I have not.

Well, thank you, sir.

People say Scorpios are highly sexed. Or that they sting you when they're mad, so watch out. I think they're shape shifters. Jamie wasn't invisible to the policeman. He had simply changed his identity.

My favorite Jamie photo: Jamie smiling in the AuSable river, right wrist flicking a fishing line.

My favorite Jamie memory: We had just hunkered into our double sleeping bag when something inordinately large ran right into the side of the tent. I knew it was a black bear. I knew this in a perfectly calm way, with a quarter of an inch of canvas between him and us and with the night wrapped around us.

Go away, bear, Jamie said in his best basso profundo. He was holding me. I could feel the sound of the words in his chest. There were a few seconds of complete silence, then the bear ambled off and we fell asleep.

Summer

A lot of people who kill themselves get drunk first. They call this liquid courage. When someone we know in AA kills him- or herself, somebody will almost always ask, *Did s/he pick up* (a drink or a drug)? Nine times out of ten, the answer is yes. Jamie was among the nine out of ten, according to the person who found him.

I've always wondered what Jamie drank before he killed himself. Since I never knew him drinking, I can't imagine what it might have been. It's kind of odd that, in five years, we never discussed what he used to drink, but I don't remember him saying whether he liked beer best, for instance, or tequila, although I'm pretty sure he knew I used to be a wino. Maybe his last drink was hard liquor, something straight and quick.

I do know why he killed himself, though. We'd talked about that a lot. He often hated being alive. And he thoroughly hated being alive in the summer. Since he'd never sincerely not considered suicide as an option, it seemed only natural that he would want to get out of summer if he could. He found the heat unbearable, pure and simple. This is my theory.

After Jamie died my shrink told me that I might have been somewhat instrumental in keeping Jamie alive for a few extra years. It didn't help too much to hear this because I felt I might have been guilty of interfering with Jamie's true life's work, which might have been suicide—that, keeping him alive, I only made his time on earth longer and more miserable. I'd abandoned him at the end, after all. How Clara Barton was that?

Jamie's depression was generous. One time he offered to kill us both, and I jumped out of bed and started dancing around so he could see how happy I was. His depression was hungry. When I was finally sure I was a lesbian, his body began to shape itself into planes and edges. His face became pointy, an isosceles triangle. People who knew us both begged me to feed him, but it wasn't really food he wanted. People said, *Have sex with him, what harm could it do?*

His depression was too kinky and magnanimous for me. It liked to act out in groups of four or more, having sex in ambitious ways. I was an almost ex-nun, for one thing. I had special powers, for another, and the imposed integrity that goes along with them. Lastly, I was as possessive as a pit bull.

I consulted a psychic a few years after Jamie died. He had trouble locating my troubled ex on the alternate plane at first. (Jamie always kept a low profile.) When he finally found him he said Jamie was still on the depressed side but was learning that life could be lighter, that by the time Jamie reincarnated he would be ready to embrace joy. I wondered how this fit in with my understanding that depression is mainly physiological, but I was glad that Jamie didn't seem to hold anything against me at least. I missed him, but I missed him when he was alive too. We'd lie beside each other after the deepest orgasms either of us was capable of, and I'd miss him. Or I'd miss someone. I thought at the time it must be him.

Almost Out

Mary P. was a fifty-something Westchester housewife I liked because she was a "good girl" like me. I never would have met her in her monied circle, much less ended up sponsoring her, which I did—a fortunate thing because we got to help each other not be so "good" as we stayed sober.

I would lose Mary as a friend and sponsee later on when I confided in her that I might be a lesbian. I'd thought it was only fair to tell her. She was a pearls and Pappagallo kind of housewife, and a Reaganite.

As it turned out she said she was afraid I was attracted to her, even though I reassured her I wasn't.

At first I couldn't figure out the whole lesbian attraction thing. I mean, I wasn't attracted to most women and I was still attracted to some men. Was I a real lesbian? I started hanging out at the Feminist Writer's Guild in Manhattan and met Ellen, who informed me that

I would have to do something about my looks if I was serious about being a lesbian. Normally I looked pretty housewifey myself, I have to admit—no pumps and pearls, but suburbanly tame. She suggested some leather, maybe a vest, black jeans, a flannel shirt, and combat boots. Exactly what she was wearing. And I'd have to get my hair cut short, like hers, never wear makeup, and act a little tougher, perhaps, or at least not so girly. *No pink, for God's sake.*

When I discovered that I seemed to be attracted to the mannish variety of lesbian the dominoes fell around the room in a perfect line, and by the time half of them had clacked down I knew I was what my friend Ellen had disdainfully called a *femme*. Politically incorrect, longhaired, lipstick wearing, with a persistent yen for a woman I'd seen once at an AA meeting in Manhattan who I'd mistaken for a guy.

Another new friend reassured me that I would have no trouble being a dyke just the way I was. That I would someday find a woman who appreciated long hair, ankle bracelets, and the art of acquiescence—in short, I needed a butch.

Oh, Closet

I was pretty sure I'd uncovered a butch in a straight West-chester County AA meeting. It was just a feeling that increased as we became friends. Madeleine had a vigorousness that reminded me of male energy. Or maybe I felt around her the way I felt around some men, a slight buzz, as if they were about to call me *Darling* and place a hand on the small of my back and I was about to feel like Jo March in *Little Women* when she met Professor Bhaer. None of these observations registered in my mid-'80s mind, however. They expanded over time like phlox in a garden, returning each year until I'd trip over another root—*So that's the way it works!*—male, female, yang, yin, gender coding and gender anarchy.

I used to sit across from Maddy at a meeting and think: I wonder if she knows she's a lesbian. Mad was the first Mensa member I'd ever met. She often said, *My whole life all I ever wanted was to be normal.* I knew I'd have to take care in the way I broke her lesbian news to her.

Maddy, I said one day after our Friday night meeting, *can I talk to you about something?* Chronically naïve, I'd still managed to pile up eight or nine years of One Day at a Times and, since Madeleine was fairly new to the program, I thought I'd tuck her under my wing a little.

What's up? Mad said.

Please don't take this the wrong way, I started. How could she? She was already looking at me as if she were my tenderest friend.

Okay, she said. She was listening.

I took a breath.

Well, I was thinking that maybe, just maybe, now that you're sober? You might find out that you're a lesbian.

I believed she was experiencing a one-eighty—a complete turn around—and I wanted her to know I was on her side. I'd seen this kind of transformation on countless occasions. The further someone got away from booze the more interesting the changes. People switched from thief to deacon, perfecta player to soup ladler, Stepford wife to college grad. I knew a woman who came into AA as a lesbian and after a year decided she was straight and married my friend Dave, plumber turned Himalayan cat breeder.

I hadn't heard the expression *come out of the closet* in 1985, but I was thinking maybe it was time for Madeleine to come out of hers.

Silly me.

Maddy almost split her jeans laughing. (She'd known since she was six.)

We went to the hardware store to buy her a new electric drill and I stood there at the cash register and pretended to be her girlfriend. It felt comforting. Like when Jo went running after Professor Bhaer and there he was, walking down the road, in plain sight, close enough to call back.

Oh, Closet Redux

I told myself and my friends that my biggest fear about coming out as a lesbian was telling my children, but, in truth, my biggest fear was that I would be murdered. And, if I didn't get murdered, an awful lot of people were suddenly going to hate me.

When I told my baby sister, the Christian fundamentalist whose husband aspired to be a deacon in one of those enormous prairie churches with a rock star pastor and who home-schooled her five kids to keep them away from Satan's snares and sodomites, she was visibly appalled. This was hard for me to take, considering I'm fifteen years older than she is and had to deal with some pretty funky diapers of hers for a while. But, then again, I was also her godmother when we both used to be Catholics. (She gave up Catholicism for "Christianity," which has always brought a smile to my heretical lips.) I suppose she had a right to be disappointed that the sacred

130

tutelage she'd received from her big sister had ended up tainted because of sex acts she obviously couldn't understand or even begin to imagine.

Aren't you afraid of AIDS? she'd asked, horrified. I'd hit her on a bad day. A (straight) neighbor of hers had been killed recently and the police were going house-to-house asking questions. My poor sister had just been through the ordeal when I showed up and told her I was on my way to hell and wouldn't be spending even a day of eternity with her.

My kids were the hardest, however. If it hadn't been for the fact that Clio's friends thought it was cool for me to be a lesbian, I'm not sure how long it would have taken her to come around. She seemed to take it as an affront to her own budding hetero lifestyle, assuming that, in choosing women over men, I was criticizing her choice, a seventeen-year-old punker with hair that fell half way down his face. Not so! I loved Luke. They looked adorable together as prom ghosts.

Sophie and I sat in the car somewhere in Sleepy Hollow. I'd pulled over to have a quiet moment with her and finally plunged in. When she realized what I was trying to tell her, her face registered true shock and a deeper pain than I was prepared to see. I felt like I had caused a kind of violence.

In essence, I had simply told the truth.

Christmas in the Woods

At possibly my poorest '80s point (as my future partner, Mars, used to say, there's poor and then there's po'), I gathered up my two daughters, packed a picnic, and drove to the Appalachian Trail near Bear Mountain with Jamie to celebrate Christmas. The kids and I had strung popcorn and cranberries that morning to use as bird-edible tree decorations. We'd planned which songs to sing, and we'd unanimously decided it was a better way to spend Christmas than going into debt over presents—and a hell of a lot more fun than using our ficus plant as a Douglas fir again.

But it was cold. And children don't do well in that kind of cold, no matter how bundled. We found our spot and draped our decorations on tree branches for the sparrows and cardinals. We inhaled our sandwiches and sang "Good King Wenceslas," who was the Duke of Bohemia, as it turns out—a fitting subject for our favorite carol. Then it was over. Clio and Sophie wanted to go home. The birds had never shown up. The sky had turned steely. It even snowed a little, but not a pretty snow, more like sleet.

I loved straddling the trail that stretched through fourteen states and wound so close to New York City. I loved the bite of the wind and the stillness beneath the soft whining of the kids. I looked at Jamie and he was red-cheeked and so beautiful, alive that day in the arms of his favorite gods. And I looked at my children, pulled between their father's Alfa Romeo and my old Chevy, his vital pregnant wife and my terribly ill boyfriend, and I saw that they were tired.

So I took them home.

But I like to imagine that the earth felt happy that day for the time we spent there. That the sun came out and dried the popcorn we'd heroically tried not to eat as we strung the kernels that morning, making jewelry for the sparrows.

Three

Jubilation, she loves me again. I fall on the floor and I laughing.

Paul Simon, "Cecilia"

Mars

I was minding my own business right before a meeting in Manhattan—Thursday night Women in the Arts AA—listening to the rats chatter in the open ceiling on Saint Mark's Place, when a man walked into the room and sat down next to me. I was fairly new to this specific group, still checking out the women's scene in the city, but I knew one thing: if a man even showed his face at the door of that meeting, those downtown women would boo him out immediately and unmercifully. Heady stuff for a good girl, yet here was a guy plopping down beside me with nary a *hey* from any of the other women.

Even when she talked Mars held on to her mystique. And, believe me, Mars could talk. Sweet talk, coffee talk, beat around the bush and the bird that's in it, talk. I'd never, I mean never, met anyone like her.

Before the meeting started she made it clear to the whole group that she was looking for a job, and they said they'd see what they could do. They liked her, I could tell, laughing no matter what she said or how she said it—she had the blarney, I certainly recognized that. I was bewitched and terrified at the same time. I embarrassedly searched my English-major vocabulary for a word to describe her energy, her looks, her mannerisms, and couldn't find anything close.

She asked me a few years later: *What did you think when you realized you were attracted to a black woman?* (Just for the record, I'm white.)

That part didn't surprise me, honey, I said, *it was the fact that you were my first bona fide bulldagger that took my breath away.*

She liked that.

After the meeting on Saint Mark's I knew I'd found who I was looking for. I was thirty-eight years old, and my rampant decade of indecision, that old familiar, was on the decline. I believed I just might make it to lesbian land after all.

West Side

My first real encounter with Mars was like a scene from *West Side Story* (the butch/femme version) where the Sharks and Jets have an unlikely operatic reconciliation. Tony and Maria find themselves face to face on the dance floor and the fire is lit. Their friends get involved right away, not rumbling, but definitely mumbling. Tony's friends warn Maria about Tony. Maria's friends warn Maria about Tony. Maria feels too pretty to care, and the other actors capitulate and dance across 14th Street against the light. Tony snakes along behind Maria and makes semi-lewd comments about her body parts. Maria joyfully ignores Tony's innuendos. Thus it begins.

I was sitting with my friends in a pizza parlor on 7th Avenue having a slice and a seltzer. The four of us had just been to a meeting at the Gay Community Center down the street and I felt bold with my girls beside me. I had girls, for God's sake, real New York lesbians.

The bell over the door dinged, and I looked up casually to see more of my AA friends walking in carrying guitar cases. Vogueing in the middle of them: the eminent Mars. We all shouted greetings as they went up to the counter for their slices, but—and, believe me, I almost did not trust my own senses—Mars came right over to me as if on some kind of mission, bent down conspiratorially, and, like a bee in my ear, buzzed: *Marry me.*

I was shocked, yet not. I'd wanted her for eons. I answered, in a flash of embarrassing unoriginality: *Watch out, I'm vulnerable.* (Maybe I needed the comfort of a cliché.)

Tony: *Will you go out with me, chica?*

Maria: *Sure!*

I knew I had her. I don't know how I knew. There was never a moment when I didn't know. If there was a missing piece to the jigsaw of Molly, it was Mars. An entire life rolling along to this moment on the corner of 7th and 14th, West Side of Manhattan, in the year of All Dominoes down: 1988.

King of the Butches

was in the second floor bathroom at the pre-renovated Gay Community Center, and the window next to the sink was wide open. I washed my hands and leaned out to watch her arrival. I could hear her coming down 13th Street. It was Father's Day, the day of our first official date. I'd been gone on a weeklong writing retreat in Connecticut and had called her to see when we could hook up.

I'd just peed three times in half an hour.

The whole time I was away I'd been in fantasy sex world—I tumbled there after Mars asked me out and I said yes. I saw wild turkeys running around the forest and thought of sex. I wrote a poem about light on oak bark and thought of sex. I stayed up at night, secretly afraid out there in the woods by myself, and slept during the day, dreaming about sex. I'd become obsessed with the flummery Mars had thrown at me during our West Side Story fling-ding and sing-a-long.

But I was cool.

She had her posse of butches with her when we finally faced off on the sidewalk, not looking at each other, grinning stupidly. She introduced me to her friends, and they appraised me and voiced their approval. They said things like: *Nice work, Mars,* and that string of *mmms* black people do best: *mmm mmm mmm mmm mmm,* emphasis on the first mmm, nice and long, and then four notes in staccato, 6/8 time. Mars was the King of the Butches. She glowed among them like the most handsome creature ever conceived to love women on this earth. I was amused at everyone's bold lack of political correctness, especially my own. I was clearly besotted, and I hadn't touched a drop of booze in eleven years.

We broke off from the group and decided to retrieve my car from its parking spot on 7th Avenue and drive it up to Harlem. As we walked we passed a church where a bedraggled middle-aged man sprawled on the steps drinking from a bag.

Hey, man, Mars said.

She went up to him and stood there for a second or two until he looked up.

Hey, man, she said, holding out her hand and shaking his with respect—

Happy Father's Day.

Helmet

I'd hooked up with Mars a couple of weeks before my planned move down from Ossining to the Upper West Side, and she offered to help.

We stopped to have a sex break on the stairs to the second floor of my apartment while we were moving me out. It was so inspiring she still talks about it to this day, but my favorite sex story from those early times happened that first night we got together at her place in Harlem.

I'd kept on with the vulnerable theme of our pizza parlor meeting, and she'd countered with her own brand of flirty bullshit until we ended up on her couch, Mars wearing a motorcycle helmet, and me hoping to hide the huge cotton underpants I'd deliberately put on to discourage myself from having sex on the first date. The helmet was supposed to be a symbol of protection for us both. The underpants were a symbol of futility.

She was lying on her back and I was on top, staring down at her through the helmet visor, and I started kissing her neck a little before she did the flip thing you always see in movies, where Tony wraps his arms around Maria and turns her over so she's on her back and he's on top, and the real sex can begin. (You may think I'm half-kidding about this, if you like.)

The reason this isn't Mars's favorite sex memory may have something to do with my drawers, since she's the one who had to look at them, but I think she'd say it's probably still her second favorite sex memory. For me, it exceeded almost a decade's worth of trips to fantasyland. It may have been the exact moment I began to think of God as Goddess.

IRT

My Manhattan apartment mate Katya wasn't crazy about Mars, or me and Mars as a team, or me and Mars having sex in my rented room while Katya padded past on her way to the kitchen. I'd rented from Kat once before over a summer of writing and Upper West Side AA. Maybe, this time, she was hoping to see more of me, or maybe she just didn't care for Mars. Mars took up a lot of psychic space. Maybe it was that competitive butch thing.

At any rate, Mars and I spent most of our time together on 119th. She'd rented a large two-bedroom garden apartment in a brownstone that she and the friend who owned it were rehabbing.

Whenever I took the red line up to Harlem, I would either change from the local to the express at 96th and Broadway or stay on the express, the number 2 or 3. Most of the white people on the express would get off at 96th, and had probably never taken the 2 or 3 into Harlem. Let me speak for myself. *I* had never taken the express into Harlem. If I'd wanted to get up there, to walk past the famous Apollo Theater or buy handmade earrings in the open air market, I'd take the local, get off at 125th, and walk east. Harlem had intimidated me before I met Mars. I always thought I was trespassing there, like, what, couldn't I just stay on my own side of the world after my ancestors and their progenitors had taken and were still taking over a major portion of it? So while I'd be sitting on the number 3 to Harlem I'd be thinking: I used to be a housewife in Westchester County. I thought that thought probably a hundred times, taking deep breaths on the IRT, before I realized how happy I was.

Ass

Reviled in the white community. Revered in the black. Come to find out, I would learn a lot about Caucasian American ethos by encountering an alternate universe right across the river from the city in Jersey that had spawned me.

Mars and I had a talk about our color difference right away. Mars did most of the talking:

Did you ever think you'd be with a black person?

Have you ever been with a black man?

Did you ever think you'd be with a black woman?

Did you ever think you'd be with a bulldagger from the projects?

Did you ever think you'd look up and see a black woman over you and did you ever think she'd do this to you?

I was not her first white woman, but I didn't care.

Mars liked to lace her fingers through mine when we were in bed. *We're perfect,* she'd say.

This was a year or two before Spike Lee would cinematically explore the topic of jungle fever, and we'd laugh with embarrassment at the way we sometimes fetishized each other. It was also a year or two before Alabama would be the last of these United States to repeal its antimiscegenation law. Not that we mattered that much to Alabama. We were chiaroscuro, not breeders. Still, it amazed me just how many folks we managed to piss off in NYC alone. It was like theater whenever we left Mars's apartment in Harlem or my room on Riverside Drive. We couldn't help ourselves. Just walking down the street together, we stuck out like heretical thumbs.

Profile

Mars liked to play games when we were out in the world together (or, as I called her diversions, performance art). Sometimes I'd go along and sometimes I just couldn't (my introvert thing), but most times I tried. One game was called THUG. She'd pretend she was a mugger and I was her target. She invented this seamy simulation because it happened so many times when she wasn't playing that she thought she'd make it into something fun for herself and turn it around on the people who were perpetrating it in the first place.

Let's say I'd be sitting casually on a bench in Penn Station. She'd come up behind me and hover, checking me out, eyeing my backpack, keeping her distance, but seeming unusually interested in me. Without fail, some well-meaning white person would catch my eye and gesture to me that I should watch my pack. I'd mouth, *Thank you,* count to ten, stand up, go over to Mars, grab her hand, and kiss her on the cheek. Then we'd walk away in a pretend huff.

Not such a cruel occupation for someone who got racially pro-filed every other day and was an obvious butch lesbian to boot.

Often she'd do it when I wasn't aware—while I was waiting outside Love's Pharmacy or riffling through CDs at Tower Records. Then I'd just roll my eyes, grab her, and we'd link arms and laugh like heteros who assumed they were happily heading toward heaven.

Soul

Most days I just loved staying with Mars in Harlem. We had a tiny backyard where we put out a card table and had breakfast on Sunday mornings when the choir belted out gospel at the church one block over. I was becoming competent at grits, and Mars made the best fried chicken livers I'd ever had, well the only, but they were memorable. We had a two-burner hotplate, that was it, and I could cry thinking about the meals we created there. (Although, without an oven, we missed our biscuits.)

One time Mars wanted to take me to a soul food restaurant up on 135th. I was hesitant because that was deep Harlem and I felt like we were pushing our interracial luck already. But we walked up the sixteen blocks and ordered our food to go—and got our message loud and clear when we got home. The waitress had emptied the saltshaker on my dinner. It was one of those times I had to keep Mars from hurting someone. Those times happened about once a day, wherever we were in the city. On one hand, it was a relief for me to be with a person who could access her anger in the time it takes to say *cheese grits*. But it was scary too, and I would often hug her to keep her grounded. *Come on, honey,* I'd say. *It's not worth it.* Sometimes my voice helped. Sometimes she couldn't hear a word I said and I'd stand against a building, hoping for an invisible cloak, while she chased some guy down the street for insulting us.

Once, she hailed a passing gypsy cab, practically threw me in the back seat, yelled *Go!* as she hit the trunk, and turned around to fist-fight with the drunk who'd just made a nasty reference to our color difference.

Sometimes the slurs were racial, sometimes homophobic. Often both. Blacks and whites seemed to hate us equally. Slurs happened in Harlem, in the East Village, near Lincoln Center, in the Bronx. I have a theory that we emitted a kind of light in those days and that it was simply unavoidable that certain people would want to put it out.

For example: Mars had just had her first orgasm with another human being, me—an incredible letting go for a butch from Brooklyn. We didn't know what the crashing at the barred bedroom window was at first (it turned out to be chunks of concrete), but it was frighteningly loud and went on for fifteen minutes while I held my lover and she simply and quietly and, extremely uncharacteristically, wept.

Parade

One day we were lounging in bed and we heard music up the street. We jumped up, threw on shorts and T-shirts, ran over to Adam Clayton Powell, and there was the African American Day Parade in full regalia heading north.

My family was a big parade family. As a Knight of Columbus, my father had often marched in local parades while we all cheered him on. I remember seeing mummers as a kid and thrilling to their amazing height and the costumes and the sound of the snare and bass. I'd been to countless Macy's parades, and I'd staggered, smashed and exhilarated, alongside revelers on Saint Patrick's Day. No one adored percussion more than I did. I was a parade fool!

But this. This was indescribable. Drums beyond my wildest. And the dancing! Whoever heard of dancing while marching? I mean, seriously. I thought back on beloved past parades and scrutinized the limits of my mock military training: nothing moving but the feet, hands ironed mid-thigh, head straight, spine erect, feeling the beat but not letting it show—like the way you're supposed to stand up at perfect attention at Carnegie Hall during Handel's "Hallelujah" chorus while your heart is hammering joyful in your chest.

What a crock, I thought, and went immediately AWOL.

Parade Redux

Mars liked her clothes to match when she went out. She would plan her outfits with admirable care, obvious affection. She'd lay everything out the night before, iron the works, creasing and steaming, and then she'd make sure the ensemble matched, hat to socks, right down to the startling underwear.

On Pride Day there were jeans, a royal blue T-shirt with a huge red, blue, and yellow Superman emblem, red socks, red drawers. Beside this finery was my own matching outfit, except for red underwear (femme style), which I did not own and would not concede, causing Mars a small amount of sincere regret. Not only did Mars like to coordinate herself—she took equal pleasure in coordinating me to match her. At first I thought this was a black thing, or maybe a lesbian thing, or a black lesbian thing, but then our white hetero friend Janet stepped off the plane from Disney World with her husband and kids, every one of them in matching sequined Mickey Mouse jackets, holding matching Goofy bags.

It just isn't me! I said to Mars, who was pushing a pair of her red socks at me. *I'm asymmetric. I like minor keys and irrational numbers.*

Mars grabbed me and pulled me over to the full-length mirror.

Look! she said. There we were in our identical Superman shirts proudly provided by Mars the day before. The words *E-Gads* and *Holy Shit* flashed through my mind. I tried to buck up.

We look cute, I said. *But I'm forty years old! What would my kids say?*

They're not here, she said, logically.

My own mother would die, of course. I took a deep breath and thought: What the hell?

Mars switched on Stevie Wonder, who always accompanied our leaving the apartment, and we danced around for half an hour. Then we headed downtown on the number 3 express out of Harlem, adrenaline pumping hard, two women with Superman emblems and matching red socks, not trying to pass as anything but crazy in love.

Mars and Sophie

Clio was in her first semester at SUNY Purchase and Sophie was still being held hostage at Harper's in Pocantico Hills when Mars and I hooked up.

This is how Sophie had come to be a hostage three years before:

Harper (1985): *Clio and Sophie want to come back to live with you, Molly, but I can only give you enough money for one.* (Harper's salary as a bond trader: Six digits.) *You can have Clio. We don't know how to deal with her anymore.* (My salary as a secretary in food service: priceless.)

Clio was fifteen at the time. She had called me and threatened to kill herself, begging me to come get her as soon as possible. I was hoping to obtain legal help, so I recorded this particular conversation on a tiny tape recorder that played back later at double speed, as if we were Disney mice. *Don't kill yourself, okay?* I'd said, like Cinderella's tiny footman.

I told Sophie that she would have to stay with her dad and she could come and sleep over with me and Clio whenever she wanted—every weekend certainly, or more often. We only lived down the hill.

Sophie didn't get it. What ten-year-old would? She barely spoke to me for two or three years after Clio came back to live with me. The first time I remember her even smiling around me was the day she met Mars. She was twelve then. We were walking down 104th Street to Katya's apartment and Mars leaned over and said: *Wanna speak Spanish, Sophie?*

Sophie frowned.

The day had been a good one—we'd hit the Hard Rock Café and Strawberry Fields—but Sophie had been freezing me out as usual, and Mars by association.

Mars had a fluent, sometimes dubious, Spanish vocabulary and few, if any, inhibitions. She was about to share her expertise with my daughter.

Sophie, she said, *say "bese."*

Sophie hesitated.

Come on: Bese.

Sophie opened her mouth and said it softly. I could see she knew what it meant.

Mars (Peter Pan) looked at me (Wendy) and whispered something in Sophie's ear. Then they looked at each other and burst out laughing. I pretended motherly offense.

Bese mi cuco! Mars said, putting one arm around me and the other around Sophie. *I swear, Moll. That's all I said. Kiss my cuckoo! Right, Sophie?*

Sophie was still laughing.

And, although I wasn't exactly included in that moment on that day, I noticed Sophie threw me a look that had the hint of a new idea attached to it: *Maybe.*

Mars had made a friend.

D. J.

Like me, Mars had also given birth in a former life: a son named D. J., now eleven years old. I often saw them together during my rare Mars sightings around the city, pre-me. Once, they were wearing matching outfits and looked like bumblebees, big and little, with a boom box.

D. J. lived with Mars's mother in Far Rockaway. He was a deep little guy, smart and imaginative. He looked just like Mars, who he called Ma, which always threw me. *Mommy.* Imagine that, I'd think, Mars was once with a man.

I was drunk! she reminded me.

Oh, the beguiling paradoxes of a butch girlfriend.

Clio Gets Sober

T'd been to the O'Keeffe exhibit at MOMA one day in October and that night got a call from Clio at college saying she wanted out, she was hitting bottom with alcohol and drugs, could she come to stay with me in Manhattan.

I'd been waiting to hear those words from Clio since she was fourteen, when I'd unintentionally caught her in an alcoholic blackout. She was still living with the two H.'s at the time and had gone out with her friends on a Friday night, called to say she wouldn't be able to come see me until the next day, then called me the next day to apologize for not calling me the night before. Ah ha! (My daughter's first tooth, first word, first blackout.)

My spiel was this: *Your two parents have it, your four grandparents have it, most of your aunts and uncles have it.*

We were looking at each other over burgers at the Ossining diner. She got tears in her eyes. *Me and Sophie?*

Very possible, I said.

But Sophie's only nine! That's not fair!

I know.

What should I do?

So I told her about Young People AA and all the help out there. (Actually, Harper and I had both been on standby to help Clio.)

Okay, honey?

Okay, Mom.

Three and a half years later she was with me at Katya's, waiting for a bed across town in a rehabilitation program.

Mars and I wrapped up dinner that Thanksgiving and brought it to share with Clio at rehab. We made enough for a whole ward of newly recovering drunks and addicts who were playing ping-pong when we clomped snow down the hall and passed out paper plates. We all sat around and chowed down: turkey, cornbread, collard greens, stuffing. Gravy over the works.

Normally, I have to say, I don't feel comfortable using the word *blessed.* It seems to imply that some are chosen, saved from the fire, raised from the dead, and some, oh well, just aren't (they must have really fucked up somewhere along the line, poor saps). I don't believe anyone's creator could or would operate that way, doling out blessings to certain kids, withholding them from others.

But this is a story of chunky cornbread and ham hocks in collards and turkey legs and yams and rich gravy with little shiny puddles of butter rising to the top. Of hungry people involved in personal events that just might have picked them up and spun them around 180 degrees until they didn't recognize where they started or who the hell they were—all enjoying a great meal on a blustery November afternoon. *Blessed.* What other word can I use?

Carving

I got a great supplemental job house-sitting for the month of August '89 at a beautiful place in Riverdale, right on the Hudson. It was the first time Mars and I ever saw a moonset.

I'd talked Mars into staying with me at the Dominicks', and one morning at about four o'clock I woke up to find her pinning me down on the bed, practically breaking my wrist. This had never happened before, but I knew intuitively that she was in the middle of a nightmare and yelled, *It's me!* several times before she let go.

I thought someone was going to hurt my mother, she said, bursting into tears. *I mean, not you, some white guy.*

The full moon was setting into the Hudson. *I didn't know the moon even set, did you?* I asked Mars later.

Not a clue, she said.

We were sitting up in bed in the room that seemed to float among the trees, and we watched the river swallow the moon and turn dark again.

I'm sorry about your wrist, Moll, Mars said. *Someone was trying to kill Belle. Jesus.*

The Dominicks' was where Mars first started to carve wood. She found a small scrap block in the basement, took out her utility knife, and carved a face into the grain. It was stunning. I'd looked at it unbelieving that Mars had had this talent for thirty-five years and was just now discovering it.

You're a sculptor, I said.

She didn't want to be a sculptor.

A wood carver then.

She didn't want to be anything that had the connotation of artist. She thought I was nuts for writing poetry, and often told me so.

How do you expect to make a living writing poems? she'd asked me for years. She sounded like my father, my ex-husband, but with an undercurrent of begrudging admiration. She loved my poems, especially the ones about her, of course, but she just didn't get, or wouldn't admit to getting, that it was my life's work.

What about your kids?

What about buying a house?

What about your old age?

We'd had this same conversation dozens of times, and now here Mars was, knife in one hand (she eventually used chisels) and any piece of wood she could find in the other—carving through the whole month at the Dominicks'. She was uncannily adept at it. Add this to her list of extraordinary musical abilities, and I had to laugh whenever she got on my case about being an *artiste*.

I wrote a poem about the morning Mars almost broke my wrist, and it came out in my first book two years later. A well-known (well-loved by me) white writer who reviewed the publication singled out that poem to remark that, in her opinion, I hadn't mined my privilege enough. At the time of the review, Mars and I had had a commitment ceremony and crossed half the country together. We'd been spat on as an interracial lesbian couple. We'd loved each other's kids and we'd taught each other lessons about gangster/nun, organized/ messy, morning person/night person, turkey legs/blackened salmon, *Rambo/Babette's Feast*. The normal stuff of relationships.

Mars was furious with the review. I got sad for a while then snapped out of it.

I've rewritten that poem a hundred times in my head. The final image rests on me, not Mars, which is what, I assume, the reviewer found so disturbing—that I would claim pain in a relationship that was culturally skewed—as if I were somehow unaware of the impact of what I was saying or insensitive to Mars's life.

Before Mars had her nightmare at the Dominicks', before she almost broke my wrist and we sat together watching the moon set into the Hudson, she'd eased two fingers inside me and held me, rocking me until I came. Then she drank every drop of me she could find. Beside us on the night table was the sculpture of a woman's face she had finished that day. An African face. I'd cried when I'd found it as a surprise under my pillow. I may not have earned it, I may not even have deserved it, yet there it was—and it was mine.

Far Rockaway

*M*y first time with Mars on the Rock:

We followed dried spots of blood down the hall in our Kente prints—Mars in a dashiki and I in African pants and black shirt. Her mother had just turned sixty and we'd been invited to her party. We looked amazing.

D. J. met us at the door and hugged me many times. He said he loved sculpture (Mars had told him she'd begun to carve wood), that sculpture was *dialectic.* He repeated the word with such authority I believed him. Later I wrote in my diary that the ocean seemed to carry away the rules. *Ocean Village is a whole world,* I wrote.

Sonny, Belle's man of many years and the father of her four youngest, showed me pictures of his children with his white wife. Belle didn't seem to mind. *They'll be here later,* she said to me over her own kids' heads.

Then she called me into the kitchen to get to know me and showed me the food she'd been up most of the night preparing. *For your own party?* I asked. I felt bad that we hadn't thought to bring food. *Sweetheart, if I don't, who will?* she said, but she didn't seem to mind about that either. There was a cloved ham, macaroni and cheese, potato salad, collards, and classic fried chicken. Oh, and pig's feet, which Belle wanted me to try.

(Sorry, Belle.)

I did take a spoonful of the gravy the feet floated in, however, and it was delicious. I think I may have managed a tiny bite of something Mars said was ear not foot.

I was the first girlfriend Mars ever brought home that Belle liked.

Mars's sisters' kids were hanging on both of us. Doogie fell asleep with his head in my lap. It was so hot his sweat soaked my leg. He smelled little and old at the same time.

Mars braided her nieces' hair. They sat before her, aged five and six, like sphinxes. Their heads bobbed with the force of her hands. *Tender-headed,* Mars called them, although neither complained.

She took me to meet her younger brothers in another room. Robert could drink a Beck's in less than thirteen seconds. He did this twice to show me. Cal was a poet. He wrote rhymed lyrics that sent chills down my arms. He wrote them out like long prose poems, but he knew them by heart, and he could make up stuff off the top of his head (an early freestyler), sometimes with a beat from his boom box, sometimes with just the beat in his mind. I loved Cal. His lyrics filled my mouth. Mars said, *He'll either be dead or famous soon.*

D. J. heard her and laughed. She smacked him playfully.

The ocean surrounded us on all sides.

Equine

Weekdays I rode the number 1 train to the end of the line, 242nd Street in the Bronx, and walked up the hill to the prep school where I still worked in the kitchen, entering inventory and counting money at the end of each day.

My best friend in the kitchen was Earl Starks, and my only friend among the preoccupied teachers was Barry Siebelt. Barry and Earl were way way out of the closet. One taught and directed theater, the other did it daily while he worked in the kitchen: Diana, Madonna, Chaka, and Earl.

My coworkers, who had known me for several years (and since I was with Jamie), were not thrilled when I told them I was gay. I came out to them in solidarity with Earl and Barry, but mostly for Barry, who, when he found out he was HIV positive, sat down in my office and burst into tears.

My straight coworkers tolerated the new me.

They even tolerated us when I brought Mars around to meet them. Needless to say, Earl and Barry adored her. She'd come up to get me after work, hang out trading insults with Earl (*the dozens*) while I counted the cash, then she and I would head back to her apartment or down to the Village for an AA meeting.

What they couldn't handle, seemingly en masse, was our announcement that we were getting *hitched*, well, *holy-unioned*.

Here's one thing my boss said: *How would you like it, Molly, if I came to work one morning and told you I had slept with my horse?*

I was officially offended, even if I couldn't see her point. I'd been living with Mars for months, had known her for almost two years, and I'd never once mentioned sleeping with her to my boss or brought up sex in any way.

Also, I'd seen pictures of the horse at my boss's home in Connecticut. He was beautiful. I felt sorry for him, so *Give me a break,* I said, and drew up a letter I presented to the school's attorney about the harassment I was receiving from management. My boss quit her insults to both me and her horse immediately.

The snubbing from the other women was more difficult to take. I've often wondered how it happened that so many kind people suddenly turned biblical on me. What I've decided is that my straight coworkers didn't so much mind if Mars and I were lovers. What seemed to bother them the most was that we thought we had the right to be a real couple, kind of like them, although this was 1990, fourteen years before the first same-sex marriage in Massachusetts, and certainly, we weren't asking for anything legal. I'd already been divorced twice, for God's sake.

All we wanted was a party!

The Broom

Our friend Chris said we could use her place. What could be better than Brooklyn in June? Dogwoods and magnolias, a block from the El? It had been ten years since I'd attended one of my own weddings—a long fraught decade for which I deserved a nuptial reward. And it was a first for Mars. She was practically psychotic with anticipation.

My parents had flown in from Illinois to attend the wedding of one of my cousins that same weekend. The times didn't conflict, but coming to ours wasn't an option for them. They declined politely. Mars's mother was not so polite, which surprised us. She wouldn't even allow D. J. to attend and told us that what we were doing was a disgrace. *No offense,* she added.

What we did: We wrote our own vows; we put together an altar with Mars's sculptures, one of my poems in a frame, and dozens of white roses; and we invited a sober lesbian minister from the MCC Church to preside.

The whole event rocked.

We went a little nouveau-Christian (we hadn't come across options yet), choosing Ruth and Naomi as our biblical role models and sharing bread with our guests, who bawled through most of the ceremony. Earl manned the camcorder, and lots of friends took stills. We both wore silk and went extreme butch and femme, at least in looks. (Mars deftly braided my hair, and I drove the rental car from Manhattan.) My kids beamed the whole time. We danced our butts off and opened presents.

Mars's sister Rose came for the reception with her two little ones. She made a big splash arriving late and seemed genuinely happy for us. We found out the next time we visited her in Far Rockaway, through Rosalie, her little girl, that she thought we were disgusting, but she showed up, as Mars pointed out. *That's something.*

There were 75,115 legal marriages in New York City in 1990 and 25,734 divorces. *Who wants to be a statistic,* Mars said, with a bridegroom's bravado.

Mars and I talked about divorce at various times over the years. *How would lesbians do that?* she'd say, kind of wild eyed. The prospect of divorce always panicked her.

Finally we decided, if it ever came to divorce (and it wouldn't!), we'd jump backwards over the broom, like the Africans who found themselves on foreign plantations without human much less legal rights. Forward, you're hitched; backward, you're not.

That day, we leapt over the broom, then hopped back on it and flew tandem home to the Bronx where ordinary things awaited us: milk in the fridge, toothpaste in the medicine cabinet, our names on the mailbox, a futon that doubled as a couch and a bed with an extra thick mattress. We'd bought it downtown in the Village in 1989. I've still got it.

Mars says I've still got everything.

Speech

Mars built a loft "bedroom" for Sophie in one corner of our studio apartment on Netherland Avenue. It was the size of a twin bed, had shelves and a ladder, and Sophie came on weekends to the Bronx from her father's in Westchester County to stay with her dyke mom and her mom's new partner, who she called her step*feather*. When Sophie was aloft in her bed you could only see the top of her head peeking out. She'd be listening to her Walkman or reading a book for school and Mars would be cleaning and straightening and I'd be cooking breakfast and we three felt cozy and close and happy.

Mom, Sophie said one day, sipping peppermint tea at the tiny table in front of the window that looked out over Route 9, *I want to live with you and Mars full time. I'm going to be a sophomore next year—that's when Clio got to do it—and I'm coming, no matter how poor we are—I don't care. Anyway,* she added, *I feel richer with you and Mars than I do with Daddy and Honor. I'll get a job! I'm moving in, that's that.*

It was a long speech for Sophie and I was impressed and warmed to my toes. Also, scared to death. But Sophie knew our financial situation. She was incredibly smart and practical. She was no nonsense. And she was right. We'd make it work.

Okay, I said, and hugged her.

I spent the next few months checking out boring boxy two-bedroom apartments in the area. We certainly couldn't afford those. Then I checked out one-bedroom boring boxes. Couldn't afford those either. The only place that looked feasible had a nice landlady who turned out to be not so nice when she said to my face that I wouldn't have to worry about *those people* moving into her apartment complex.

Those people? I said, and snapped my check out of her hand. *I am one of those people,* I said, over my shoulder, not exactly knowing who the undesirables were, but not waiting to find out either.

We moved to Chicago.

Impulsive, yes, but not as crazy as it sounds, partly because housing in Chicago in the early '90s was cheap (for a New Yorker), and my family lived about an hour northwest. On previous trips Mars and I had been to the gay AA club on Clark, so at least we knew a few folks there. Neither of us had jobs, of course, but what did that matter to trusting souls like us?

I left the harassing coworkers behind and drove a fifteen-foot Ryder truck the familiar eight hundred miles directly into the Heartland. Mars said good-bye to family, friends, box cutter. In May 1991 we leapt from the Hudson highlands to swampy Chicago and prepared a place for Sophie to fly to in August.

We were eager, naïve, and arrogant—New Yorkers in a foreign land.

Chicago-Style

To this day Chicago is mysterious to me, an onion patch of paradoxes. So beautiful in spring yet so bone ugly in winter. So tall downtown yet with a short city's complex. So culturally rich yet so suburbanly satisfied.

I apologize to all Chicagoans and Chicago lovers, I truly do, but please don't get me started on Chicago pizza.

When Mars and I arrived in the Windy City—as our entire troupe of friends insisted on calling it a thousand times before we left and for years afterward—we were invited for a special dinner at Betsy and Lara's apartment in Ravenswood, a North Side neighborhood. They were a friendly lesbian couple Mars and I had met at the Newtown Alano Club, which had recently moved to a new space on Clark Street, and they insisted on introducing us personally to Chicago stuffed pizza.

Well, we certainly loved pizza—the lovely crisp crust thrown over the head of a practiced Italian and caught on a fist, the chewy mozzarella, the tomato sauce dripping down your forearm as you folded a hot slice and took that first anticipated bite. It was a staple in New York. You could consume four food groups while walking from Ray's to the subway on 96th Street.

Chicago-style was waiting for us when we arrived at Betsy and Lara's. The elaborate confection on the dining room table had flaky crust, four different kinds of cheese—including gruyere, Lara told us proudly (gruyere, for God's sake?)—and mouthfuls of tangled spinach.

After years of living in Chicago and bitterly missing New York pizza cut in adult-sized triangles, not forty-two kiddie-sized squares, I realized that I had to start thinking of both deep-dish and thin-crust Chicago pizza as a different genre altogether. Pizza cake, for instance; pizza crackers might be another possibility. My mother used to make us English muffin pizzas. A spoonful of Hunt's from the can, a paper-thin slice of mozzarella, and a sprinkling of dried oregano—yum. I was open. I was an adventurer.

But that night the two of us were bereft.

There was nothing to do but hang together. And punt.

Funnel

So there we were, ex-pat Manhattanites knocking around in two thousand square feet of space, a block from Sophie's school, down the street from the north branch of the Chicago River with its mallards and herons, and right in the middle of a Christian Korean neighborhood at the end of the Ravenswood El. Jim and Ivan, our landlords, lived downstairs and were gay. Hooray! No hiding necessary.

The day the funnel cloud came ripping up the Chicago River, Mars and I were busy at opposite ends of the apartment. Jim and Ivan had given us the combination to the basement—*Just in case,* they said—promising it would be the safest place. So when it turned pitch black at four in the afternoon and I heard a roar like an approaching jet and the front windows sprang open and drafts of my poems flew around the room, I screamed for Mars and we ran for the basement with the combination in hand, hearts drumming furiously.

What the hell are you doing?

Jim had come down the back stairs to find us fumbling with the lock. We were pretty sure we were going to die.

We need a flashlight, I said, stating what I thought was obvious. We couldn't see a damn thing.

Come on in and have a drink, he said, nonsequiturially.

Uh, Jim, didn't you feel the TORNADO go over just now? (This was Mars, and she was controlling herself, believe me.)

That wasn't a tornado, he said, in a pitying tone. *Jeez, you two. You need a drink.*

That was our first and last personal Chicago funnel cloud. It ripped down trees along the river then went on to do damage to the flora at a nearby college campus where I would soon teach fundamentalist Christian kids how to write a poem and use the word *fuck* nongratuitously. I would take them to do a reading at Barnes and Noble in Evanston, and we would be asked not to use profanity because the poetry was automatically pumped into the children's section, where Mars was engrossed in her favorite kid's book and missed the whole event.

Everybody Poops! she reminded me later over cheese fries and grilled chicken sandwiches, philosophical as always. Then:

Except in the Midwest!

Lake

On special occasions, Mars and I would walk all the way to Lake Michigan. It couldn't console us like the ocean, but it was the biggest thing around, and we needed something really big once in a while to lean against.

Mars wore her man clothes and I linked my arm through hers and we'd head across Chicago toward the lake. *East!* we'd say, setting out on the same foot, reminiscing, delighting in the sounds of our New York voices.

Tawk to me, she'd say.

Cawfee, I'd say.

Fuckin' A!

There's a moon here too, I'd say, trying for assimilation. *Look!*

Sure—but it rose from the Atlantic, she'd say back.

Mmm. I miss salt!

And the truth of our situation—that tricky displacement, that prairie-flat reality—would make us stop and hug right there on Montrose.

We'd once walked all the way from Harlem to the Brooklyn Bridge on a summer night soon after our commitment ceremony. I'd insisted Mars wait until we were halfway across the bridge before we stopped and turned to see the shock of Manhattan's lights strung chaotically from tower to dock.

I'd wanted to hear her breath catch in her throat then see it blossom into a big Brooklyn grin.

Pie

Mars and I weren't picked on as much by the general public in the Windy City. We stayed home more, for one thing—we weren't out running wild on the subways or El trains like in New York. It was too damn cold! Mars didn't sing to me in perfect fake French on train platforms. She didn't hide behind columns and pretend she was going to mug me. We had an old diesel engine Caddy and rarely even took public transportation. We rode in style holding hands on worn leather seats.

We often passed as a straight couple when we went out. This wasn't always deliberate. Mars had become less of a kid in Chicago. Or maybe we wore so many layers to keep warm, people couldn't tell the difference. Or else we'd just become an old married couple.

I don't want to be an old butch, Mars often said.

You'll be fantastic and adorable.

You know what I mean—a crusty old butch.

But I didn't know what she meant. I thought it was a lot easier to get old as a butch than a femme in our society. And I loved the way butches looked no matter how old they were.

Remember: Black don't crack, I'd remind her. Something she'd taught me early on.

Yeah, we just get bloated as hell, she'd snap back.

Our favorite *passing* moment was at Baker's Square, a chain restaurant in Rogers Park known for its pie.

I ordered the sugar-free apple and Mars ordered the regular apple, and the waitress said, *Thank you, sir,* to Mars after we ordered, and then, *You're welcome, sir,* after she'd brought us our pie.

Mars didn't always feel overjoyed about being mistaken for a man. She seemed to want more control over it—and sometimes, I just didn't know which way it was going to go. But that night she was thrilled.

Kiss me, she said, quietly, leaning in.

Kate and Allie

To this day, Harper and his wife Honor have no idea I've been with Mars (admittedly, off and on) for the past nineteen years. When we left Manhattan for the Bronx, and then New York for Chicago with Sophie, Honor told my kids that she thought it was so cute the way Mars and I moved around together—like Kate and Allie, she said, which was a sitcom with Susan Saint James and Jane Curtin about two single moms who combined households to save money. The show was entertaining, but Mars and I were a bit chummier and, although I was relieved that H. & H. never guessed our secret identity when the kids were of kidnapping age, it was always kind of a bummer, and, well, infantilizing.

Kate: *Coming to bed, dear?*

Allie: *Soon as I finish hammering these nails into our new barn, move the horses in from the north pasture, strip off my tool belt and boots, and take a hot shower, darlin'.*

Kate: *Want some company?*
Allie: *Sure.*
Kate (later, shower gel in hand): *Let me wash your back, handsome.*

Mars actually preferred long baths to showers. I'd peek into the fogged-up bathroom to see her surrounded by bubbles and sunk down in the steaming water, head back against a special pillow she'd bought surreptitiously at Crabtree and Evelyn. She often fell asleep in the tub, water cold or drained out, chin on her chest. *Come to bed,* I'd say, but sometimes she'd stay there, a mermaid-man, nodding and murmuring, *Soon.*

Work

There were so many positive things about Chicago—housing and jobs, lilacs in spring, pumpkins on stoops in autumn (the reduced vandalism shocked us)—that we didn't know why we always felt strange the eleven years we lived there. Sometimes way too strange, like we were from an extinct planet or exiled in the Midwest for a reason we had yet to ascertain—and always at least a little strange, as if we would be going home any moment when we'd finished our "assignment." The Jesus billboards, the smiling faces, the assumption that the world is a friendly, happy place. These things boggled the hell out of Mars and absolutely terrified me while also inspiring me to write my ass off (two and a half books' worth of poems). I think I was writing letters (sending signals) to the mother ship (too much Spielberg).

Our job luck didn't start right away. Mars bounced around from hardware store to construction, and I worked for my father on the

South Side and in the suburbs selling books to schools that first year. The job relied on my being a morning person, which I was not, and a salesperson, ditto. I'd make it to my first school by 9:45 instead of 7:45, eek out what business I could by the end of the school day, then head home. My writing had become as inescapable as the two hundred some odd overcast days Chicago is famous for. Everything confronted me—the clouds, the lake, the Jesus billboards. *Write about me!* it all insisted. *You'll die if you don't, my pretty.*

I went to my new counselor, George the Jungian, who often fell asleep while I was pouring my heart out to him, and told him I needed to quit my job at once and find something more suited to me. You don't say something like this to a Chicagoan. He couldn't even compute the concept at first. When he finally realized I was saying that I was really going to quit my job, he told me, flatly, *No.* Jungian or not, he obviously didn't care about my dreams.

No? I said.

Never quit a job until you've found another one.

I'd heard that one before. I was forty-two and I wasn't actually from Pluto. Plus, I'd lost so much sleep over the whole business, analyzing options, worrying about everyone. I needed something fresh, something an industrious transplanted New Yorker might say to me, like: *Carpe diem, Dorothy Parker. You could set up a poetry booth near the Wrigley Building and write poems on demand for people on their lunch hours. You could play keyboards in a rock band. You could get a MasterCard!*

I quit my job. I told my father and my therapist that I was going to do phone sex and write poetry. We all hoped I was kidding, and then I got word (the following week) that I had won both a National Endowment for the Arts fellowship and an Illinois Arts Council grant, which enabled me to take a year to write.

My father said: *But what will you do when the year is up?*

George fell asleep as I was relating how I felt guilty that I hadn't sent any of my homoerotic work to the NEA. I went home immediately and wrote a poem about a chicken.

Chicken

I threw that poor bird, which had been marinating in olive oil and herbs, across the entire length of the kitchen, where it lodged beneath the door of the dishwasher, one leg poking out dramatically (and pathetically). This leads me to the following questions:

Did this action in 1994 foreshadow my switch to vegetarianism in 2006?

Was I pissed at George the Jungian?

Was I anticipating George, the Bushes?

Did I hope to hit Mars with the chicken or did I simply hope to inspire myself to write a poem?

Did pitching the chicken trigger a newfound freedom in me?

How long after the chicken slid beneath the dishwasher did Mars and I:

a. laugh hysterically?
b. cook and eat it?
c. start to unravel?

Was Sophie home or was she breaststroking in the over-
chlorinated high school pool that would turn her fingernails blue
with asthma?

Does anyone remember this besides me?

Alter

My name isn't really Molly and this worries me. Do I think I'm protecting myself? And why did I pick a name I don't particularly like and that some might recognize as a character in a famous, complex novel? What's worse is that I recently passed Ruth Meek's mailbox in Benzie, Michigan, and decided that Meek would be Molly's last name if she ever needed one. Molly Meek. That's just wrong.

I've changed most of the names of the people in this story for absolutely no reason except that as a poet I know I will never write a novel, and I wanted to see what it would feel like to have characters. You always hear about how characters do whatever they want in a novel, and I wondered if that could be true for a memoir as well. Sure enough, Mars said recently that the day we had our first date in 1988 she was waiting for me at the Gay Community Center and watched me walk down the street, not the other way around. Maybe

Molly just went ahead and did what she wanted in that chapter, regardless of the facts. Molly remembers peeing three times in half an hour but I don't remember peeing at all.

Some names from my life I kept, like Bruce, the excellent kisser. And I really did call my grandmother Mom Mom, although her name was Frances Angela, and if I had become a nun I was going to be Sister Frances Angela unless they'd made me take a male saint's name, in which case I'd have been Sister Francis of Assisi. I once put Mom Mom in a poem that I wrote with one of my collaborators, Alphabet (a name he chose himself), during hurricane Frances. Alphie has lived his entire life in Florida, which is where I live now, so obviously Alphie's been waiting for Molly to show up for a long time so they could write poems together.

Now I'm getting Molly confused with a character other than myself. Perhaps she is complex after all. I like to think so.

Some Girls Noir

The move to Chicago was catastrophic for Mars and me. Neither of us was able to predict it because she'd never lived outside of New York. We were both thrown off axis, and the Clark Street lesbian AA meeting (where the women rarely used profanity, and when they did—*My stars, Pollyanna!*—they apologized!) proved treacherous for us.

One Tuesday we entered the meeting together, and a snickering clique checked us out and rated us on the butch-femme scale. (This is NOT your typical AA group.) We were both *tens*. Mars liked the verdict, but I was embarrassed. Did I ever wear hose and pumps? No! Had I ever had a pedicure? No! (Well, not yet.) It was true, Mars held doors for me, but I held my own in the world of jobs and traffic, not to mention natal family.

I noticed that a lot of the women seemed unduly—sometimes sneakily, sometimes obviously—interested in us as individuals, whether we were married or not. The butches would watch me from afar, circling, making eye contact. The femmes were downright flirty—they'd barge right up to Mars, acting so junior high I couldn't believe it. Then one of them would turn, all normal and AA, and say to me: *It's hard being new in town. Here's my phone number. Don't hesitate to call.*

Like I was going to reach out to a woman who wanted to sleep with my partner.

That was the dicey social environment. At home it was worse: tectonic plate-ish. I was holding on to the sides of our sloshing boat. Mars seemed to be dismantling like Sargasso seaweed. Her grief stretched for eight hundred miles—the distance between Chicago and home—and I despaired that I would not get her back to New York before she disappeared.

October

I'd always wanted a tree house as a kid, and the leaf-lush sun parlor at the front of our apartment came close. It was the same year all the elms were dying in Chicago of a disease no one could control, the month a famous gay photographer called to ask if he might photograph me in my writing studio. When he met Mars, he wanted her in the picture as well, and she and I stood together in the sunlight, not touching.

By my birthday at the end of the month we were far and officially apart.

The Leap

*E*very few years the lens on the camera I'd aimed at myself would change and I'd see my navel differently. This was disconcerting. When the Alcoholic lens snapped into place, I told my friends: *Oh, my God, I'm an alcoholic.* Everyone was like: *We knew that.* I was like: *How did you know?* They: *You told us already, remember?*

Then the Divorced lens snapped into place. For about two years I withdrew from Stepford syndrome. I was the first to be divorced in my family, mother's or father's side. I was young and stupid in some pretty hefty ways: e.g., I'd never written a check in my life. *What will I do?* I asked everyone. *What you've always done,* they said. I was handing out my worldly possessions, silver trays and pewter goblets Harper and I had gotten as wedding gifts ten years before. My friends filled large sacks with the spoils of our marriage, and said: *You will put one foot in front of the other.*

Never one for slogans, no matter how useful, I cringed.

The Poet lens revealed a crafty demon that threatened to swallow me and my innocent offspring. To identify, on however small a scale, with fools and suicides or even the Tillie Olsens I'd admired, I had to believe in Tinker Bell, in mystery and intuition, and in my ability to provide for myself and my kids as I dragged them back and forth from Ossining to Neverland. I'd unwittingly tripped over my essence.

Then the Lesbian lens:

I'm a lesbian!

So?

I'm a fucking lesbian!

I wonder how it is that some people seem to hop on a track at birth and follow it faithfully until the end, while others blow about like dandelion seeds. At twenty-eight I had first decided to turn my life over to the wisdom that had created me and brought me to a place where I might begin to love myself. The decision was a huge risk, of course (*Oh, the Places You'll Go*), and not made lightly (*Oh, the Thinks You Can Think!*), as it was whenever I remade it. Still, it was merely a decision to leap, not the leap itself, and by the time I was ready to take the leap, I'd already leapt, so there you have it.

Everyone said, *Amen, you big dyke.*

With special powers, I added.

The Broom Redux

This October Clio will celebrate nineteen years without a drink or drug.

I will celebrate thirty-one.

Sophie will celebrate five.

This is, of course, as my Irish grandmother, Frances, used to say while downing a quart of warm Rheingold, puffing a nonfiltered Chesterfield, or handing me a whiskey-soaked maraschino: *God willing.*

Mars and I decided (and have continued periodically to renew our un-vow) not to jump backwards over the broom, although we've mostly stayed separated. We've morphed into friends then back to lovers then friends again on numerous occasions. It's an interesting way to love someone: this liminality, this keening. I personally have no clear vision of the subjunctive whatsoever, and, to Mars's sometimes dismay, I actually don't mind our flipping coin, our slated peace and tension. We're both still sober, after all, which makes absolutely everything possible.

Here we are at the Best Pride Parade Ever, Chicago, 1994 (*almost as good as African American Day in Harlem*). We've patched ourselves up long enough to go public, and we're standing on the corner of Broadway and Buckingham when Sophie, her hetero eighteen-year-old self, marches past with NARAL, a pro-choice group she joined in high school.

Mars and I know Sophie will be solidarity marching. What we don't know is that NARAL has joined up with the Dyke Drum Corps, so she's surrounded by women with snares and a bass and homemade percussion instruments, who, whenever the drumming stops, kiss each other on the lips.

There's my beautiful daughter, smack in the middle of queer society at its most Windy City flamboyant, drum strapped around her waist, sticks raised. Mars and I jump in and dance with her down Broadway, surrounded by dazzling, outrageous, Chicagoland women.

That is what I've chosen as my penultimate image. I hope you like it.

Epi

I would like to tell you the names of the famous people I've seen at AA meetings over the years, mostly in NYC, a few in Chicago, and elsewhere. But I won't. *Who you see here, what you hear here, let it stay here.* Hear, Hear!

I read in a book about Oppenheimer that the same admonition was posted at the gate of the Los Alamos Laboratory in New Mexico while scientists concocted the first atom bomb in the early 1940s. It makes sense. What I don't know is, did AA get that slogan from the bomb makers or was one of the bomb makers an early member of AA who brought the slogan from a meeting to his work site one day? I've asked Clio to check this out.

Most ideas in AA are borrowed. That's not a slogan, just a fact, and it's fine with me. I believe fervently in recycling—most of the time. There are exceptions, like the time I was on a mild rant about the way 99 percent of the meetings in Chicago closed with the Lord's

197

Prayer (this was in the mid-'90s). Based on my experience, there seemed to be a pretty large number of Christians in Midwest AA who hadn't registered the fact that there were those in their midst whose spiritual practices did not include the Our Father. To me it was kind of a *DUH* thing. So I said to this cute butch at my women's AA meeting (Mars and I were separated at the time): *I wish we could close the meeting with something else besides the Our Father. Like the Serenity Prayer,* I added in a spirit of compromise. *It's a little more generic.*

What do you mean? she said.

I mean, you know, something else besides the Our Father—for other people besides Christians.

The Our Father's not a Christian prayer, she said. *It's an AA prayer.*

The Lord's *Prayer?* I said. Then: *Where do you think they got it?*

From the Big Book, she said.

Nobody's perfect, I thought, and I took her home and slept with her.

A Note on Anonymity

*Anonymity is the spiritual foundation of all our traditions,
ever reminding us to place principles before personalities.*
Tradition Twelve, Alcoholics Anonymous

As a spiritual principle, anonymity has enabled me to start and sustain an extraordinary new life, to meet courageous people and not know or care where they're from or what they might do for a living, and to remember that I am no more and no less a citizen of this world than anyone else. So it is understandably with some trepidation and after much thought that I publicly break my own anonymity. (Others in the book have agreed to fictitious names, sometimes ones they chose themselves.)

It is also with profound respect for the recovering anonymous communities that my name appears here. I do not seek to promote my lifestyle or attract others to it. I am not a spokesperson for AA or Al-Anon. Neither am I a spokesperson for the LGBTQ community or lesbians everywhere. I am simply me, a mother, a poet, sober, and queer, and I wish my readers their own revelations on their own wild paths of truth.

LIVING OUT
Gay and Lesbian Autobiographies

Joan Larkin and David Bergman
SERIES EDITORS

Raphael Kadushin
SERIES ACQUISITIONS EDITOR